# LESSONS *from the*
# SCHOOL *of*
# SUFFERING

A Young Priest With Cancer
Teaches Us How to Li

**REV. JIM WILLIG**
With Tammy Bundy

## ST. ANTHONY MESSENGER PRESS
Cincinnati, Ohio

Cover illustration and design by Constance Wolfer
Photo on page viii by Ron Rack; RackPhoto.com
Interior design, electronic format and pagination by Sandy L. Digman

ISBN 0-86716-455-7

Published by St. Anthony Messenger Press
www.AmericanCatholic.org
Printed in the U.S.A.

# CONTENTS

✝ TO JESUS, *who is my way, my life and my truth* (John 14:6).

✝ TO OUR HEAVENLY MOTHER MARY, *who is a source of great intercession and consolation.*

✝ TO MY LOVING FAMILY, *who helps me carry this cross of cancer every day, every step along the way.*

✝ TO MY SPIRITUAL FAMILY, *the parishioners of Saints Peter and Paul Parish in Cincinnati, who faithfully love me and pray for me.*

✝ TO ALL WHO ARE SICK AND SUFFERING, *as well as those who care for them.*

# FOREWORD

**R**ECENTLY I WAS DINING with an architect friend and his wife. Styling himself as a somewhat cynical realist, my friend challenged me by remarking that by the time midlife comes around, people don't change. We just stay locked into the personalities, patterns, convictions, biases, likes and dislikes that have come to define who we are. I told him that I believed this to be true for many but not for all. He pressed me to name some individuals who had changed in midlife. Immediately I responded by naming Mother Teresa and Cardinal Joseph Bernardin.

My architect friend pushed these public examples aside and said, "Yeah, sure, they're the exceptions. But do you personally know anyone who has *really* changed and become a different person in the middle of their life?"

Without missing a beat, I responded, "Yes! Father Jim Willig! I know for a fact that Father Jim is not the same person he was a year ago. His struggle with cancer is reshaping his personality and making him into a saint."

Today is the Feast of All Saints, and I stand in the conviction that God has called all of us to become just that—saints. And who are the saints except those who have allowed God to form them and love them into holiness?

Usually this forming and loving is a direct result of suffering. This is the process I see taking place in the heart, mind and soul—the person—of Father Jim Willig. It is the process, we hope, at work in all of us. But in the "school of suffering," some of us are placed into a classroom for accelerated learning.

Long ago, Saint Irenaeus wrote, "The glory of God is a person fully alive." It is a mystery of the deepest order that as renal cell cancer has eaten away at Father Jim's body, he is becoming in the eyes of those who know and love him "a person fully alive." There is a freedom, a joy, a wisdom, dare I say—a holiness—in Jim that has always been in the embryonic state. This holiness is only now emerging with a power that was not present previously.

I have been a Jesuit for thirty-two years and a spiritual director for many different people during this time. I count it one of the greatest gifts of my life to serve as spiritual director for my friend, Father Jim, as he walks this path on which God leads him. Throughout Jim's journey with cancer I have witnessed the most extraordinary changes in the heart and soul and person of a man I thought I knew. Do people change in life? Some do; many don't. It's clear that people don't change automatically.

Suffering is no guarantee of holiness. Some people walk through their education and learn little, while others seem hungry to learn. So it is with suffering: For some people it can be an invaluable teacher; for others it can crush a person into self-pity.

I have witnessed Father Jim's openness to learn from his life experience. I have always admired Jim's eagerness and desire to learn. I know few Catholic priests who have put more time and effort into learning to be a more effective preacher of God's word than Jim Willig. He has always been hungry to learn more about Scripture. It is with this same zeal that Father Jim has sought to learn from the cup of suffering that Jesus has asked him to drink.

This book is a record of one man's account of his "yes" to deeper intimacy with God. This volume testifies to what that "yes" has cost Father Jim. More importantly, he records how richly blessed he has become.

Father Jim provides us with a textbook. God's grace will determine when and with whom we will study. But this much is certain: Suffering in life is inevitable. None of us is getting out of here alive! What we do with this suffering and whether it teaches us anything is a choice we all must make.

Many, many people have questioned God's wisdom in allowing this young priest to suffer with cancer. Jim Willig, well loved in Cincinnati, is a gifted homilist, an excellent Scripture teacher, a pastor with charisma and charm matched by few. With the priest shortage such as it is, how could God fail to see how much Father Jim is needed to continue his work in his parish and around the country?

I don't presume to know the mind of God. But Father Jim's reflections begin to help us shift our gaze from the cost of the cross to the gift of God's grace. Jim is not afraid to let his soul be seen, to name his fears and frustrations, and still cling to his deep belief that the Lord will lead him safely through this storm.

Each of these life lessons has cost Father Jim a healthy chunk of tuition. I don't believe any one of us will fully appreciate what Jim has learned until such time when the Lord enrolls us or someone we love in this same school of suffering. For those already enrolled in the school of suffering, this book will provide an assurance that we are not alone, that suffering does, indeed, have meaning and purpose. For the rest of us, *Lessons From the School of Suffering* provides an opportunity for a bit of advanced study, so that when that registration form arrives on our doorstep, we will, like Father Jim Willig, be open and ready to change for the better.

*J. Michael Sparough, S.J.*
*Feast of All Saints*
*November 1, 2000*

# INTRODUCTION

**S**OME THINGS YOU JUST KNOW. It was that voice we all have inside us to guide us, even though we don't always listen. But this time I was actually listening. And so it was that I scheduled an appointment to meet with the priest of my new parish.

Three months earlier, shortly after I had started attending Saints Peter and Paul Catholic Church, the pastor, Father Jim Willig, announced that he had renal cell cancer. My intense reaction to this news left me confused. I barely knew this man. Why would this diagnosis touch me so deeply? I felt the Lord was telling me something here, but I didn't know what it was.

I then wrote about Father Jim's unfolding story in my column for *The Cincinnati Post*. But, somehow I knew that wasn't all there was to it.

Some things you just know.

When Father Jim returned from his surgery after his kidney was removed, I felt that same "something" telling me to go to him and offer my assistance. And so I set up that appointment. "I think the Lord wants me to help you," I boldly informed this recovering priest who hardly knew me.

Kindly, Father Jim thanked me and graciously suggested that I might be able to help him with writing for an Inspiration Line he was starting. The Inspiration Line turned out to be a telephone hotline where people could phone in daily to receive an inspirational message. We did, indeed, work together on this, and it was a success. But still, I knew that was not all

1

that I was being called to do.

Some things you just know.

Then one day I had a meeting with Father Jim to discuss that Inspiration Line. It had been a rough day for him due to receiving the news that his cancer was spreading. Upon leaving our meeting, I felt that forceful "something" stop me in my tracks and make me say to Father Jim, "I think the Lord wants me to help you write a book about your cancer journey."

Father Jim humbly replied, "No. I don't think anyone would want to read anything I have to say right now." He was physically and emotionally drained. But he politely added, "I will pray about it, though."

After I left, as I sat in my car, I too, prayed: "Lord, if this is simply my thought, let it go now and I won't bring it up again. But if it is *your* thought, please put it in Father Jim's heart, too."

The very next day, Father Jim pulled me aside after Mass and said words to me I will never forget. "You won't believe this," he excitedly began, "Reverend Howard Storm, who is a close friend of mine, called me this morning and said, 'Jim, I don't know what you'll want to make of this, but last night I had a dream. In this dream, the Lord told me to tell you to write a book. And he told me to tell you not to worry about not being a writer. He's going to send you one.'"

Of course, I believed it.

Some things you just know.

*Tammy Bundy*

# CHAPTER ONE

# The First Day of School

*...they strengthened the souls of the disciples
and encouraged them to continue in the faith, saying,
"It is through many persecutions that we must
enter the kingdom of God."*

ACTS 14:22

I FELT DRAWN TO GO TO THE CHURCH. Of course, since I am a priest, that statement may not seem unusual. But there was absolutely nothing usual about this particular church or place.

This church was the Church of the Holy Sepulcher, and I was in Israel leading a pilgrimage. This church contains the very site where Jesus died on Calvary and also where he was then laid in the tomb and rose from the dead. I had always been fascinated by the fact that these two most sacred sites of brutal crucifixion and glorious resurrection are only about twenty yards apart and under the same roof.

And so it was that I felt drawn to come to that sacred site

3

every morning at six o'clock to pray before the pilgrim day began. Little did I know that those early morning prayers served to turn the page on a chapter of my life that no one willingly wants to begin.

In my prayer at the Church of the Holy Sepulcher, I would ask Jesus to teach me about his death and resurrection and what they mean in my life. It was at this sacred site that our pilgrim group celebrated Mass one day. I was privileged to preach at this Mass. I shared with everyone about my sister, Laura, who had recently discovered she had breast cancer. I witnessed how her cancer had brought her closer to the Lord. Despite her suffering through chemotherapy and radiation treatments, as well as the anxiety and uncertainty of her illness and life, she spoke of this as a time of bitterness and tenderness—a time when she felt both so alone and yet, so loved.

The lesson I highlighted in my homily was that the way we suffer often becomes the way we experience God's blessing in disguise. Granted, at times, our suffering seems to be a good disguise, indeed. But just as the Church of the Holy Sepulcher contains both the place of Jesus' death and the place of his resurrection, so often in our lives, the very situation that causes so much pain or sorrow is the very place we can experience God's blessing and new life.

It proved to be somewhat prophetic that I shared those thoughts at that holy place where Jesus died and rose. Shortly after returning from the Holy Land, in fact, just days after, I went to my doctor who ordered a CAT scan for me. When I returned for the results of this scan on July 6, 1999, the doctor said words to me that are forever burned in my memory, "You have renal cell—kidney—cancer."

When Dr. David Krick shared this news, I was so shocked, I could hardly believe it. Was he really talking to me? Maybe I had misunderstood. But then he invited me to see the X ray that showed my right kidney enlarged with a ten-pound tumor—the size of a football! I would later come to understand that renal cell cancer is often referred to as a silent and hidden

4

cancer: It hides itself inside the kidney, which is encased in the ribcage, and there are rarely any symptoms.

I felt so confused and overwhelmed; all I knew was I needed to pray. So, I asked Dr. Krick if he would mind if I said a prayer right there in his office. He graciously agreed, and I offered this simple prayer, "Dear Lord, I place my life in your hands. Amen." Seldom had prayer seemed so intensely heartfelt.

As I walked out of the doctor's office, I knew my life would never be the same. At age forty-eight, I found myself back in school. Only this school was the school of suffering. This school requires classes virtually no one willingly signs up for. The tests are hard. The assignments, at times, seem impossible. Nevertheless, the lessons I have learned in this school have taught me more than I ever dreamed I would know. You might even say, they could fill a book.

Alone I drove back to the rectory where I live at Saints Peter and Paul Church, and I couldn't help but think, "This must be why people shouldn't drive after receiving bad news." My mind was on the road ahead of me, but not the road I was driving on.

Everything seemed as if it were happening to someone else. How could I have cancer? I had always been blessed with such good health. Just a few months before, I had suspected something was growing in me, and this suspicion initially led me to my personal physician. After thoroughly examining me by probing, touching and listening with his stethoscope, my doctor concluded that there was nothing wrong that he could detect. He mentioned that he could send me for a CAT scan, if I was really worried. I remember saying, "If you don't think anything is wrong, I feel no need to look for trouble." But two months later, the trouble had found me.

As I headed back to the church, I recalled how each morning for the last several weeks, I would pray in church, standing before the altar while looking at Jesus on the cross. I would place my hands and my heart on that altar and I would offer my life to the Lord. I imagined that maybe the Lord would want to use me in a special way—over and above how he was already using me as a pastor and a priest. I even told the Lord I would offer whatever he would want, regardless the sacrifice or suffering that may be involved. I just wanted to give my whole life to Jesus for the greater honor and glory of God and for the salvation of souls. Little did I realize what that would mean. (Someone once warned me, "Be careful what you pray for!")

I soon arrived back at the church. While standing before the altar, I remembered the exact prayer that I had been offering daily, the prayer of Saint Ignatius:

> Take, Lord, receive, all my liberty, my memory, my understanding, and my entire will.
> Give me only your love and your grace—that's enough for me.
> Your love and your grace are enough for me.
> Take, Lord, receive, all I have and possess. You have given all to me. Now I return it.
> Give me only your love and your grace—that's enough for me.
> Your love and your grace are enough for me.
> Take, Lord, receive. All is yours now.
> Dispose of it wholly according to your will.
> Give me only your love and your grace—that's enough for me.
> Your love and your grace are enough for me.

Now, having entered this new school of suffering, I stood before the altar, and I prayed again. But this time my prayer was less pious. It was simply, "Jesus, this is not what I meant! What are you doing? Is this your answer to my prayer? If it is, can we talk about it?"

Then I began to cry quietly—not just because I have cancer, but because I didn't feel I was ready to give my entire life unconditionally to the Lord as I had earlier prayed and promised. I truly wanted to live this prayer and promise, but I was overwhelmed by my human emotions of fear and anxiety. As a priest I had seen so many parishioners and friends suffer and die from cancer, and I didn't feel ready or willing yet to be such a martyr. As I stood again before the altar, filled with both holy desire and human fear, the last verse of that prayer came back to me.

> *Take, Lord, receive. All is yours now.*
> *Dispose of it wholly according to your will.*
> *Give me only your love and your grace—that's enough*
>   *for me.*
> *Your love and your grace are enough for me.*

With those beautiful words still echoing through my heart, I said "yes" to the Lord. Because I had cancer, my life was truly the Lord's to do with as he will. From that moment on, I knew only one thing for certain: I do not know what my future holds, but I know who holds my future.

It was time to start sharing this news with others.

One of the first persons I shared my news with was Rose, a member of our parish staff who was assisting me in initiating the Network of Care, a program to assist and care for the sick, suffering and the elderly in our parish community. The first meeting of the Network of Care was to take place the same afternoon that I went to the doctor. I told Rose I would be back in time from my appointment for this important meeting. Due to my lengthy doctor's visit, however, I missed the meeting. Later, when I shared with Rose that I had renal cell cancer, I told her how ironic it was that *I* would be the first patient in the Network of Care!

For me there is no better example of a "network of care" than my family. And that evening I had to face the difficult task of telling them, my good and loving family—two parents and ten brothers and sisters—what I had just learned. Earlier, they had been called and told that I needed to tell them something. Except for my two sisters who live out of town, everyone came to our parents' home to hear what I had to say.

As a priest, I am quite accustomed to presiding at Mass

and services, at meetings, and, frankly, just about anywhere out of habit. That night was no different. Taking charge of the family meeting, I came right out and said that I had just learned that afternoon that I had cancer and that I was placing my life entirely in God's hands. Later my family would comment that it was as if I was presiding at a news conference.

I couldn't really fool my family, however. Sensing my fears and realizing the severity of this diagnosis, they immediately gathered around me in a circle of prayer and support. Although I had hardly begun to feel the burden of this life and death situation, I felt tremendous relief in knowing that my family was with me all the way.

We prayed and cried and, somehow, actually laughed about me being the least likely person in the family to have cancer. It was at that moment that I realized the only way I would get through this school of suffering would be with the help of God and others. But still, I had no idea yet what the requirements were for this school.

## LESSONS

✚ Suffering can be one of life's best teachers. Every difficult situation invites us to take a class or course in the school of suffering.

✚ Suffering can be a blessing in disguise if we are willing to accept it.

✚ It is wonderful and good to offer our lives entirely to the Lord, but we need to be prepared for anything to happen.

## ASSIGNMENT

✚ Try not to dread suffering. Believe that it is not the worst thing that could happen to you.

✚ Try to accept every problem and all suffering as opportunities to learn and grow. When faced with suffering, ask yourself, "What can I learn from this?"

✚ In difficult times, pray, "Lord, I place my life in your hands."

## PRAYER

### THE PRAYER BEFORE THE CRUCIFIX

*Most high,*
*glorious God,*
*enlighten the darkness of my heart,*
*and give me*
*true faith,*
*certain hope,*
*and perfect charity,*
*sense and knowledge,*
*Lord,*
*that I may carry out*
*Your holy and true command.*
—Saint Francis of Assisi

CHAPTER TWO

# The Student Body

*"Are any among you suffering? They should pray...*
*Are any among you sick? They should call for the elders of*
*the church and have them pray over them, anointing them*
*with oil in the name of the Lord. The prayer of faith will*
*save the sick, and the Lord will raise them up..."*
**JAMES 5:13-15**

**E**XACTLY ONE WEEK AFTER that first family meeting, I called yet another family meeting. This time I needed the support of family and friends even more because I had returned to the doctor for further CAT scans and learned that my cancer had already metastasized and spread to my right lung. I was extremely disappointed—more correctly, devastated—to hear this. If the cancer had been contained to the kidney, I could have undergone a simple procedure to remove the kidney and been healed from cancer. Now, however, I was faced with having to undergo difficult treatment after surgery. Worst of all, I had already read that renal cell cancer is rarely curable once it has metastasized.

As I shared this awful news with my family, they once again expressed their total support for me and they encircled me in love and prayer. We had never before felt so close as a family. We were one in heart and mind and spirit. Then we all agreed, "No more family meetings for awhile!"

For the night before my surgery, some kind friends in the parish and my family planned a Mass to ask for God's help and healing. A large number of people wanted to attend, so we had to hold the service in the church parking lot. Over two thousand people prayed for me there that night.

My best friend, Michael Sparough, S.J., came from Chicago to preach at this Mass. He proclaimed the well-known passage from John's Gospel, chapter 21, where Jesus asks Peter, "Do you love me?" In this passage, Peter answers, "Yes, Lord. You know I love you." And Jesus answers, "Feed my lambs." Again, a second time and also a third, Jesus asks Peter, "Do you love me?" Peter keeps saying yes and each time Jesus reminds him to "Feed my lambs. Feed my sheep." Along with Peter, I silently said, "Yes, Lord. You know I love you."

But the Gospel continues and Jesus tells the most strikingly foretelling message to Peter that absolutely hit home to me. He said, "'I tell you, when you were younger, you used to fasten your own belt and to go wherever you wished. But when you grow old, you will stretch out your hands, and someone else will fasten a belt around you and take you where you do not wish to go'" (What he said indicated the kind of death by which Peter was to give glory to God.) When Jesus had finished speaking, he said to Peter, "'Follow me.'"

In his homily, Father Michael reflected on how in my recent life the Lord has certainly tied a belt around my waist and has led me to places and situations where I certainly would have never wanted to go. In fact, even being lead to Saints Peter and Paul Parish is certainly a work of providence that I had not planned. But, as always, the Lord knew what was best for me when he led me to this beautiful and humble parish where people would so much gather around me, pray for me, support me and love me throughout this whole ordeal of my struggle and battle with cancer.

That night in the parking lot as I looked out upon the two thousand people who had gathered to show me that support, I felt so amazed at this outpouring of love and faith. Filled with the spirit of the crowd, I announced during the Mass, "Anyone who is as sick as I am shouldn't feel this good!" I felt so uplifted by everyone's prayers and love that I didn't think the journey to come would be that difficult. Unfortunately, however, I still had much to learn.

On July 20, 1999, I entered Cincinnati's Bethesda North Hospital for removal of my right kidney with the ten-pound tumor. My entire family met me at the hospital to be with me and pray with me. My good and close friend, Reverend Howard Storm, came also to lead me to the operating room, where I remember him praying Psalm 23. All during this time, I actually felt "The Good Shepherd" with me. Certainly my family and all my friends, especially Rev. Storm, who stayed with me and prayed all during the operation, revealed the Lord's presence to me.

I awoke hours later from the surgery, with my family gathered around me in the recovery room and sharing with me that all had gone well during the procedure. My brother excitedly came over to me and said, "Good news, Jim!" I groggily focused my attention to ask what had been discovered to be good news. "Your picture made the front page of *The Cincinnati Post!*" came his reply.

While this may not have been the good news I could have imagined, I was touched to hear about the wonderful newspaper article that recounted the two thousand faithful friends who had joined together to pray for their pastor during the parking-lot Mass. I was honored to hear about how God had used this situation for the first of many times to give a witness to the wider city and community.

This was only the first of many lessons the Lord would teach me—that the more humble I would become, the more God would raise me up as an example and witness for God. I quickly realized that the school of suffering required a crash course in humility.

My time in the hospital passed rather quickly. I spent only five days there—three in the intensive care unit where I received excellent care. There was one moment, however, that proved a bit precarious. I was in the intensive care unit under close observation when the anesthesiologist came in and informed me that I was breathing too slowly. I said to him, "Do you want me to breathe faster?" thinking that my respiration rate had already increased with that announcement. He explained that the epidural medication that was so wonderfully slowing down the pain was also, not-so-wonderfully, slowing down my rate of respiration. He needed to remove the epidural.

The doctor asked me how I typically dealt with pain. I answered that I never was particularly fond of it. As a matter of fact, during my infrequent precancer doctor visits, whenever a doctor asked if I was allergic to anything, I sometimes answered, "Yes. I'm allergic to pain." Now I was about to get a major dose of what we all hope to avoid!

I doubt that I am much different from most people in our society who are faced with pain. I had never had to deal much with pain because our society does everything possible to mask or minimize or eliminate it. We witness everyday the massive efforts by a multimillion-dollar industry to kill pain.

But during that transition from epidural to alternate pain medications, I was in excruciating pain. I had never in my life felt such physical agony. I started to feel as if I was living a rerun of my surgery, only this time I did not have the benefit of any anesthesia. I actually felt I was "under the knife"; I could physically feel a knife stabbing me in my abdomen and back.

At the moment when the pain was at its absolute worst for me, I cried out to God for help like Jesus cried out on the cross. Within a minute, an angel of God came to me. Her name was

Rosalie, and she happened to be one of the hospital chaplains. This was one of many similar incidents throughout my time at the school of suffering. Often, when I have gotten to my lowest point—feeling completely down and out—the Lord has sent someone to help me. This time, Rosalie was that angel of the Lord. She held my hand and explained exactly what was going on and what I might expect in this time of transition. Her calm presence gave me strength and I sought Rosalie's counsel often to help me through the continuing physical and emotional pain.

Asking for help was not an easy lesson for me to learn. It was humbling for this minister to let someone else minister to him. I'm not alone in this mindset. So many hurting people in the world never call for help. Where do they turn instead? Some turn to drugs for relief. Others turn to alcohol to mask their pain. In each of these ways we deal with the *symptoms* of what we are feeling and not the *causes*.

Once I became willing to let others help me, I became so aware of God's presence. The presence of my support system during my hospitalization constantly reminded me of how blessed I was. While in the ICU, at least one person was always with me praying for me. It was so touching—and such a profound teaching! It reminded me to always ask for help and prayers.

The lessons from the school of suffering are humbling. The humble truth is we all need a lot of help in life with our problems and struggles. We must first recognize that we need help and then we must ask for it. This is real humility—to ask for help and to be open to receive it. If only we ask for help, God will provide it. God's response to our prayers will come through family, friends and professional people.

Perhaps an ancient proverb says it best: "When the student is ready, the teacher appears."

## LESSONS

✦ Humility is a prerequisite for learning and growing.

✦ Humility helps us recognize that we all need help in life to deal with problems and difficult situations.

✦ Humility allows us to receive and work with the help that God provides through our family, friends and professional people.

✦ We need to address not merely the symptoms of our problem, but more important, the root of our problem.

✦ God's angels (helpers, messengers) surround us. We want to be open to them.

## ASSIGNMENT

✦ Talk about your problem or situation with someone you can trust.

✦ Develop deep friendships that can offer reciprocal support.

## PRAYER

### PSALM 23

*The LORD is my shepherd,*
*I shall not want...*
*He leads me in right paths for his name's sake.*
*Even though I walk through the darkest valley,*
*I fear no evil; for you are with me;*
*Your rod and your staff–they comfort me.*

# CHAPTER THREE

# Homework and Tests

*Then Jesus told his disciples, "If any want to become my*
*followers, let them deny themselves, take up their cross and*
*follow me. For those who want to save their life will lose it,*
*and those who lose their life for my sake will find it."*

**MATTHEW 16:24-25**

WHEN I WAS RELEASED from the hospital, I was fortunate to recuperate for a couple of weeks at my parents' home since I would need special care while recovering from surgery. During that time, I began my first cancer treatment: immuno-therapy, a specific cancer therapy for those with renal cell can-cer. It consists of a mixture of two drugs, interferon and interluken 2, given by injection. When a person begins this therapy, he or she experiences extreme pain because the body initially reacts quite violently before it gradually adjusts to the drugs. And so, after each early injection, I would go into what is called the "shake, rattle and roll" syndrome—appropriately named because upon receiving my first injections, my whole body literally would shake for about a half hour or more. This reaction reminded me of a movie that I saw in which someone overdosed on drugs and went into convulsions. Even though it was only a movie, I found it too painful to watch someone suffer like that. Experiencing this "shake, rattle and roll" syndrome was agonizing for me as well as my family, who had to watch me suffer.

Shaking, however, wasn't the only side effect. Following that reaction, I then would experience a fever upward to 102 degrees for the next three to four hours. During these fever times, I honestly wondered if this "cure" was worse than the sickness.

While this, indeed, was excruciating to go through every day, I understood that my cancer was my cross, and my cancer treatment was my way of the cross. I desperately needed this focus, this higher purpose, to help me make it through the long hours of treatment and physical suffering.

Each evening at this stage of treatment, members of my family gathered around my bed at my parent's home and prayed the Rosary through those terribly difficult times. The Rosary soon became a comfort to me, reminding me that the Blessed Mother, Mary, was with me. Just as she stood beside her Son when he was on his cross, she stood beside me, helping me carry the cross of cancer.

While my heavenly mother stood beside me, so, too, did my earthly mother. Every night while recuperating at my parents' home, my mother and I shared a simple ritual: Mom would sit at the foot of my bed and massage my feet. This gentle and loving gesture always reminded me that Mother Mary was at the foot of the cross of Jesus when he turned to his beloved disciple, John, and said, "Woman, here is your son" (John 19:26), thereby giving his mother to John and at the same time, giving her to all of us. From that day on, John took Mary into his home. This image from Scripture gives me great comfort. It is there for us all. All we need to do is to invite Mary into our hearts and homes to help us, especially in our times of suffering.

My time of suffering with the immunotherapy was limited. My body eventually adjusted to the therapy, and I was able to return to my parish in September. It felt good to be back home. The entire parish could not have been more welcoming and more loving. I was greeted with a standing ovation at my first post-surgery Mass. The parishioners embraced me with their spirit of love and concern as they encouraged me to continue to take great care of myself. One of the best treatments for any disease surely is lots of love!

I tried to take care of myself through my daily treatment of immunotherapy, and I continued to receive this interferon and interluken mixture for several months. When I returned to my oncologist, Dr. Brian Mannion, I was eager to see if all my hard homework had paid off. As with every school, I had to take more tests. More CAT scans were ordered. Soon, I heard that the immunotherapy had not worked. The cancer not only was still in my lungs, but it had also grown in size and number. There were now more tumors in my right lung than there were previously.

The doctor suggested that I consider a mini-bone marrow transplant that would require a marrow match from one of my siblings. I was confident about my prognosis at this time, knowing that the chance of one of my ten brothers and sisters being a match was one in four. The morning of the testing came and each of my brothers and sisters informed me that he or she wanted to be the one who matched me. I was devastated to hear that none of my siblings was a match. I went to my parents and asked, "Tell me the truth. Was I adopted?" Soon, the crushing realization that maybe there wasn't a treatment that would cure me set in for my whole family as well as for me. Unable to hold on to the hope of a surgical cure, we simply held on to our faith and each other.

Immediately, it was decided to try a different drug: thalidomide. As a cancer treatment, thalidomide stops the blood flow to the tumors, which in turn ceases the growth of the cancer and causes the tumors to die. As a moment of comic relief, before I could receive the thalidomide prescription, I had to sign a release to promise I would not get pregnant. Would that everything else could be so certain! I was told that thalidomide would be a somewhat kinder and gentler treatment: All I had to do was take several pills each day. Although fatigue is the side effect of thalidomide, I figured I could handle that. For an active person and pastor like me, however, continual fatigue proved to be another heavy cross. Without much energy, I found it difficult to do the many things that I had previously done and taken for granted. For this reason, the day-to-day tasks of running a parish while fatigued and coping with the uncertainty of cancer sometimes overwhelmed me.

It occurred to me that I was being given a glimpse of what life is like for the sick and suffering as well as for the elderly. I began to develop a greater empathy for these people who struggle with their physical weakness and the hardship of not being able to do what they once did almost effortlessly. Throughout this school of suffering, I have constantly been reminded that I have so much to learn.

As I struggled to learn these lessons, I discovered that one of the best places for me to learn is before the cross. Every day I try to pray before the cross. I must say that I have, indeed, learned more meditating in front of the cross of Christ than I have learned from any book I've ever read, except perhaps, the Bible.

One day as I meditated before the cross of Christ, I began questioning the Lord: "Why is it that I have cancer? And why did it have to be renal cell cancer that offers such little hope of any cure? Why do I have to suffer so much? Why? Why? Why?"

In the silence of the church, I could hear clearly in my mind the words that the Gospel of Matthew had reported Jesus saying to his disciples, "If any want to become my followers, let them deny themselves and take up their cross and follow me"

(Matthew 16:24-25). I let those challenging words sink in a bit and then I responded honestly to the Lord, "Instead of being your follower, how about we go back to being just good friends?" There is something in each of us that naturally resists the cross and the sacrifice that life sometimes asks of us. It was then that I realized Jesus has many good friends, a church full of them. But I wonder, "How many followers does Jesus have?"

To follow Jesus means to deny your very self and sacrifice your life. This teaching goes against our human tendency and the way society always urges us to look out for number one. Jesus tells us we must let go of number one. Or better yet, we must rethink who number one really is.

And so I pray about this and try little by little, day by day, to consciously unite myself with Jesus on the cross. As a Catholic, making the Sign of the Cross often became a rote way to begin and end a prayer. My hands were moved, but my heart was not. Now the Sign of the Cross has become a heart-felt reminder that I am "signing my life" over to the Lord.

One day, when I thought I was alone, I prayed in church. While making this offering before the cross, a parishioner came up to me, put her arm around my shoulder and prayed, "Dear God, please heal Father Jim. And give me his cancer."

I was incredulous. I looked at her, and then back to the Lord and quietly prayed, "If she insists, Lord, hear our prayer!" Later I was able to pray, "Lord, rather than give my cancer to her, give her heart of love to me—the love that prompted her to deny her very self and pray in such a loving way."

Over the months that I have lived with cancer, I have had other people say interesting things to me in an effort to support me, such as: "Don't worry, Father. God will heal you because we need you here," and "I just know that God will not let you die."

At times like that all I want to say is, "Have you looked at a crucifix lately?" If anybody was needed in the world, it was Jesus. If anybody was good, it was Jesus. If anybody didn't deserve to suffer, it was Jesus. And yet God allowed his son to suffer and be killed in the most hideous way, in the prime of his life and ministry.

I silently wanted to share with these well-intentioned people that the only guarantee I have is that God will always be with me and take care of me. This is how I also explain it when people ask why God gave me cancer. I have to admit that I have never felt that God gave me this cancer. It is true, though, that God allowed this cancer to happen. I believe God allows suffering to happen to bring about a greater good. In fact, what we first perceive as bad, upon later enlightenment, we realize is often a gift, a blessing in disguise.

The crucifix is the perfect sign of that paradox where God allows something so bad in order to bring about a much greater good—namely, our salvation. The more I prayed with my feelings, questions and doubts, the more I came to see an image of Jesus on the cross. With one arm nailed to the cross, Jesus lovingly reaches out with his other arm, embracing me and drawing me closer to him, to experience his divine love that led him to sacrifice his life.

There is absolutely nothing good about suffering in and of itself. As a matter of fact, Jesus spent much of his ministry healing people and alleviating suffering. Nevertheless, there is much good that suffering can bring about if it brings us closer to Christ. Therefore, the most helpful thing I have learned in my bitter suffering is to unite myself with Christ on the cross, who unites himself with me on my cross. At the times of my most intense suffering, when the hurt is so deep I cannot even find the words to pray, all I can manage to do is to hold onto a crucifix or cross, thereby holding Christ, who is holding me.

In the months following, I continued to need to be held by Christ. After six weeks of the thalidomide treatment, I once again was scheduled for a series of tests to determine if this course of action was making the grade. Once again, however, I failed another test. The cancer had grown.

I cannot fully put into words how agonizing it was to hear this news that nothing seemed to work: The debilitating immunotherapy didn't work. The efforts for a mini-bone marrow transplant didn't work. The exhausting thalidomide therapy didn't work. A much healthier nutrition and vitamin regimen didn't make any difference. Nothing was stopping this cancer from growing.

My oncologist now recommended a new course of action: a combination of thalidomide and chemotherapy. I soberly was informed that there was less than a ten percent chance of this treatment working. I kept reminding myself each day, however, that I had a one hundred percent chance of the Lord taking care of me no matter what happened.

Discouraged for so long, I was uplifted by God's gracious timing and the most thoughtful and unusual action of Archbishop Daniel E. Pilarczyk of Cincinnati, who requested through a monthly "Clergy Communication" newsletter that all priests and parishioners in the archdiocese pray for a miracle for me through the intercession of Bishop Frederick Baraga. Bishop Baraga had been a priest in Cincinnati in the 1800's, who later became a missionary and bishop of the Upper Peninsula of Michigan. I was so touched by the idea of this saintly bishop interceding for me. It certainly couldn't hurt to have friends in high places! But mostly, I was touched by this extraordinarily loving request of Archbishop Pilarczyk as well as the extraordinarily loving response of those who prayed for me. Thousands of people throughout the Archdiocese of Cincinnati—people I will never be able to meet and thank— were praying for me, for my cure.

One of the great joys I have experienced with this cancer is when people come up to me and offer me their prayers. These moments are truly the silver lining in this cloud of cancer. When someone tells me he or she is praying for me, I feel it is an answer to my tremendous need. Such an outpouring of love and prayer is a miracle in itself.

This outpouring of love even found its way to Rome when a friend of mine managed to have a private audience with the pope at the Vatican. During her time to greet the Holy Father, my friend handed him a photograph of me and said, "This is one of your priests. Please pray for him. He needs a miracle." The pope nodded and blessed this picture of me. I was very moved when my friend shared this story with me. Then she showed me the photo she had given the pope to bless. It was a photo that had been taken of me on that pilgrimage to the Holy Land. I hadn't shaved for a few days, I was wearing a Palestinian headdress, and I was standing in the middle of two women, my arms around each of them. I'm sure the Holy Father must have looked at this unshaven, turban-wearing priest with a woman on either side of him and understood that, indeed, I needed help!

The prayers of so many people, from family and friends and parishioners to the thousands of people whom I have not met and even the pope himself, have touched my soul in a way that I cannot fully define.

Despite so many setbacks in treatment, I have persevered with my own prayer. Each day, I offered myself again at the altar where I first offered the prayer of Saint Ignatius: "Take, Lord, receive." By doing this, I would daily place my life in the Lord's hands. Each time I heard more devastating news about the growth of my cancer, I would go again before the Lord and pray, "Lord, my life is in your hands." The only certainty I can hold on to in this school of suffering is: "I do not know what my future holds, but I know who holds my future."

## LESSONS

✝ It is okay to ask "Why?" of God, others and ourselves.

✝ We should expect suffering as part of life, and learn from it.

✝ When life tests us, we need to remember that the only failure is the failure to learn and grow from the experience.

✝ We should give ourselves permission to feel whatever we feel.

✛ God allows suffering to happen to bring about a greater good.

## ASSIGNMENT

✛ Look at and learn from the cross of Christ.

✛ Unite your suffering with Jesus on the cross.

✛ Share your feelings openly with someone.

## PRAYER

### HAIL MARY

*Hail, Mary, full of grace! The Lord is with you; blessed are you among women, and blessed is the fruit of your womb, Jesus. Holy Mary, Mother of God, pray for us sinners now and at the hour of our death.* Amen.

CHAPTER FOUR

# Prayer in School

*[Jesus said,] "Ask and it will be given you; search and you*
*will find; knock, and the door will be opened for you.*
*For everyone who asks receives, and everyone who*
*searches finds, and for everyone who knocks, the door*
*will be opened. Is there anyone among you who, if your child*
*asks for a fish, will give a snake instead of a fish?*
*Or if the child asks for an egg, will give him a scorpion?*
*If you then, who are evil, know how to give good gifts to*
*your children, how much more will the heavenly Father*
*give the Holy Spirit to those who ask him?'"*
**LUKE 11:9-13**

PRAYER IN THE SCHOOL OF SUFFERING is not only allowed, it is absolutely required.

Without a doubt, prayer has been my greatest source of strength in times of my greatest weakness. It has been my foremost source of consolation in times of desolation. It has given me more relief than most medicines I have taken.

Prayer definitely has a healing effect. None of us will ever realize the tremendous importance and significance of prayer. Prayer changes everything because of its power to transform us.

Very early in my cancer treatment, the Lord taught me that the greatest prayer is the Eucharist. The Lord made me understand that my mind, my body and my spirit need constant, daily nourishment. It was here, at the table of the Lord, that he also taught me the finest food for my soul and the strongest medicine for my spirit is the Eucharist. It is in the gift of Communion that Christ, himself, comes to us.

For this reason, understanding my great need for Christ, I made a promise to the Lord that everyday I would celebrate the Eucharist no matter how weak or sick I would feel. And every day when I receive Jesus at Communion, I always pray, "Jesus, may your body heal my body of any physical cancer or spiritual cancer (sin) that I may be one in you." It is then that I always feel so blessed.

But I cannot say that prayer is always easy. Nor does it always feel good. Just as it has been a source of consolation in times of desolation, sometimes it seems like a source of frustration in times of desperation. Often, when we need to pray the hardest, it becomes the hardest time to pray.

I admit that I have followed a daily discipline and devotion of prayer for virtually all my life. I believe I have, indeed, grown and matured in various methods and ways of prayer over these years. And yet, when I entered the school of suffering, I felt like a beginner again. I felt that I was starting in the preschool prayer program, learning a new way to pray.

Before my cancer, I had already developed the habit of praying from the heart. In this way, I would converse honestly and openly with the Lord about anything and everything in life. For the most part, I enjoyed prayer and tried to adhere to the practice of a daily holy hour of prayer with the Lord. During this time, I would share with my God whatever was on my mind or in my heart.

After I was through talking, I would try to take time to listen to the Lord speaking to me in the silence of my heart, in the words of Scripture and in my reflection of the events of my life. In this way, I felt I was not just saying prayers, but I was allowing the prayer to arise from deep within me.

But upon entering the school of suffering, I learned that this former way of prayer was not adequate. It didn't take long for me to understand that I was being invited to relate to the Lord at a deeper level, where I had not yet developed that more intimate way of communicating with him. At this deeper level of prayer, the Lord taught me some elementary yet profound lessons on prayer.

Just as Jesus taught his disciples to pray, "Our Father," he taught me to pray more simply and confidently as his child. The Lord has taught me that just as a young child will ask his or her parents for something, the parents, out of love, will always listen and respond. That response, however, will not always be "Yes" if that is not the wise and loving thing to do.

The young child is quite confident that he knows what is best for him, just as we often think that we know what is best for us. But it would be a fundamental mistake for us to assume that we know what is best for us when we pray. For just as no two-year-old child knows what is best, we cannot know what is best.

How many times will a loving parent say "No" to a child because it is the loving and right thing to do at that time? Or how many times will the parent respond, "Not now," or "Not this"? But, nevertheless, the parent does listen and respond in some way. When we don't get what we are praying for, however, we are tempted to say that God doesn't answer our prayer.

But in these latest lessons of life, I have sensed that the Lord is teaching me to be a better listener in prayer. It is a mistake to assume that God doesn't answer simply because it is not the answer we wanted. God always answers each and every prayer. Sometimes, however, we're just not listening.

Imagine that a patient goes to the doctor. After explaining what is hurting, the patient then gets up and leaves before the doctor has a chance to even respond at all. When the patient gets home, she will say, "Hey! That doctor didn't help me at all!" Or what if that same patient stayed for the doctor's diagnosis and received advice and medicine from the doctor. When she got home, she didn't take the advice or medication. Still, she complains that the doctor is no good.

How many times do we "say our prayers" and then leave, without giving the Lord a chance to respond to us? And God, the Divine Physician, most likely is saying, "Hey! Wait a minute! Come back here. We haven't even begun to talk yet."

Prayer is a conversation, a dialogue. Yet how often have we "said our prayers" but didn't take time to listen? Like the patient who didn't take the doctor's advice, how many times have we felt that we know what God wants us to do, but we didn't take that advice either?

Maybe God is telling us to go to church more, read the Bible more, do volunteer work, turn off the TV. But we ignore those thoughts because it is easier for us to think that God simply is not answering at all. But God always answers. The sad thing is, God gets blamed for an awful lot. And the truth is, we need to take responsibility.

Staying with that example of a doctor and a patient, think about how a doctor diagnoses you. Ninety percent of the time, a patient will talk about the symptoms. But the doctor knows that to truly help you, he needs to get to the root of the problem. That is step one in the healing process. So the doctor orders many, many tests. Only in this way, can he get to the root of the problem.

And so it is with God in prayer. I believe that most of the time when we go to God in prayer, it is to discuss our symptoms. We say, "I get so upset. My husband (wife, boss, kids) drives me crazy. This makes me so mad. My life is so hard." God says, "Well, let's talk about it. Let's look into it." This is where God helps us through the Holy Spirit, because the Holy

Spirit gives us "in-sight"—sight within.

Sometimes God will want to do radical treatment, getting to the root of the problem. Most people, however, just want to talk about the symptoms. But God is at such a deeper level. We may think that God is not with us. But the fact is, we are not there with God. God is always with us—and God is always listening.

Of course, as the loving parent, God answers our plea perhaps with "Not now" or "Not this." And just as a child constantly lets his parent know what his needs are, so too, must we keep bringing before the Lord our deepest desires and needs.

We must learn from a child in order to pray with their complete childlike candor and innocence—fully expressing to the Lord what is in our hearts. However, we must not pray childishly—throwing a tantrum when it appears we do not get what we want. Sometimes when we don't get what we want, we assume God doesn't care.

There is a great story about a man who came to God complaining. He said, "Lord, why don't you take care of the hungry in this city? It is such a problem." And this man was wise enough to hear God respond, "That's exactly my question for you."

What I have learned is that very few people have developed the discipline and the capacity of praying deeply. This has to do with a problem communicating. I have a hunch that the majority of all conversation that takes place in a family is about day-to-day practical things. "Honey, did you take out the trash? Remember the soccer game is at six tonight. Your mother called."

These are basic logistics of life. But how often do we—not just couples, but all of us—ever say, "Tell me what's going on. Not your agenda, but what is really going on deep in you." How often does that happen? Not very often. If that is how we communicate with one another, do you think we communicate any differently with God? We must learn to pray deeply.

The Lord has taught me that prayer makes an unbeliev-able difference. Just as a parent will sometimes do something for a child simply because the child asked, so too, will the Lord respond to us because we have come before him with our needs and are open to his help.

When I was a little boy, we didn't get an allowance, so I didn't really have any money. I was actually a rather religious kid—I know that may not surprise many people. So when we would go to church, I always wanted to light a prayer candle, but I couldn't afford to because I didn't have the dime that it cost back then. So, I would, instead, light the candle for just a second, saying a quick prayer. And then I would blow it out—thinking that maybe I would get just a little credit for lighting the candle. This worked for a while until the priest one day said, "Who is the one lighting all these candles and not paying for them?" It occurs to me that that is how we sometimes go about our prayers. We hardly get started, then we blow it.

Like any parent who gets frustrated with their children be-cause they don't listen, the Lord must get frustrated with us. That is why it is vital to bring all our cares to the Lord who cares for us. But we must be humble with childlike acceptance in praying first and foremost that what God knows to be best will be done.

To pray otherwise would be foolish. For, sometimes the worst thing that could happen to us would be to get what we ask for. To forget that would be to act like a spoiled child.

This is why, when Jesus taught his disciples to pray, he taught them to pray first as a child to a father. And secondly, he taught them to pray "Thy will be done" before they ever asked for their daily bread.

Jesus not only told us to pray this way, he also showed us how to pray by being the best example of perfect prayer. In his darkest hour, in the Garden of Gethsemani, at the time of his worst suffering, Jesus prayed as a son to his Father in heaven. He honestly prayed that if it could be possible, that this cup of suffering would pass him by.

In other words, Jesus asked his Father for exactly what he felt and truly what he wanted, which was, "Don't let me suffer anymore."

But in the same breath, in the same sentence, he also prayed, "Father, not my will, but your will be done." This model of prayer became for me an icon of how I am learning to pray in my own hour of agony in the school of suffering.

Coincidentally—or as I like to say now, there are not coincidences, but "God-incidences"—during this suffering in my life, someone gave me a beautiful picture of Jesus praying in the Garden of Gethsemani. I often find myself praying before that image. It has led me into praying from a level that is much deeper than praying from my heart. It has helped me learn to pray from my innermost soul.

Like Jesus in the garden, sometimes my deepest prayers express themselves in tears. These tears have expressed far more than mere words could ever communicate. They express my fears, my hurts and my longings from a place deep within me I had rarely entered before. It is there I learned that I am like a two-year-old child who doesn't have any idea of what truly is best. I simply know I need help. I need to be loved. I need to be saved. The depths of these feelings were never previously given a voice in my more "adult" prayers.

It is during the depths of these prayers when I sense the Lord holding me and helping me and responding to me, often without ever answering any of my questions. It is at this precious place of prayer that I have been learning about a healing that is far deeper than I had been previously praying for. It is here, in the depths of prayer, where my heavenly Father has taught this little child how to care for his soul. And my soul senses the blessed assurance that there is only one thing necessary and that is that I remain one with the Lord in love. All the other anxieties that fill my mind and heart matter little as long as I remain one with him in love.

The difficulty, of course, is that I do not remain in those precious moments of deep prayer. Too many times I find myself anxiously concerned about so many things that I find it hard to be at peace. I keep sensing that I am being called—as we all are called—to sit at the feet of the Master. This is where I am reminded, again, that only one thing is necessary. And I can then find, once more, my only true peace. In those true moments of peace, I can honestly say it matters little to me whether I suffer much or live a long or short life. All that matters is that I remain one with Jesus.

The Lord is teaching me in the school of suffering how to live in his presence continually. I assure you, I have never spent much time in this classroom before, but it is the greatest place of peace.

## LESSONS

+ Prayer is our greatest help in times of our greatest need.

+ God always responds to our prayers, although it may not be the answer we want.

+ Prayer does not force the hand of God to act in our favor, but it should open us up to God's will.

+ We bring our needs to God, but ask for God's will to be done.

+ Jesus taught his disciples to pray as a child to God the Father, and so, too, should we.

## ASSIGNMENT

+ Pray: "Lord, teach me how to pray even as you taught your disciples to pray."

+ Pray. Take time to share with God whatever is on your mind and in your heart.

+ Pray. Take time to listen to God's response.

+ Pray, especially when you receive Jesus in the Eucharist.

# PRAYER

## OUR FATHER

*Our Father, who art in heaven, hallowed be your name; your Kingdom come; your will be done on earth as it is in heaven. Give us this day our daily bread; and forgive us our trespasses as we forgive those who trespass against us; and lead us not into temptation, but deliver us from evil.* Amen.

# CHAPTER FIVE

# Guidance and Peer Counseling

*"When the Spirit of Truth comes, he will
guide you into all the truth."*
JOHN 16:13

ONE OF THE MOST COMMON FEELINGS of people who have cancer, or who are facing some other serious illness that enrolls them in the school of suffering, is feeling we have lost control of our lives, which is a basic human need. With cancer, it's as if all of a sudden, not even knowing how it happened, we have lost the remote control to the TV screen called our life.

Before I walked into the doctor's office and entered the school of suffering, I was in control. In this new life with renal cell cancer, I want to hold the remote control, too. But I am not in control of anything: my schedule, my emotions, my body, my future. This can leave a person feeling incredibly vulnerable, dependent and confused.

When that confusion struck me, I felt desperate. It's amazing how this desperation shows itself. I began attending healing services. I visited visionaries. Someone sent me curative dirt from New Mexico. I looked at it and thought, "What am I, crazy?" Then I rubbed some on my chest—just in case.

I found myself doing things that before I would have found to be totally irrational. Someone gave me water from Lourdes. I drank it, thinking that was the closest I could get Lourdes water to the cancerous tumors in my lungs. When people gave me medals for this saint and that saint, I collected them all in a bowl. I realized if I were to wear each of the medals I have been given by thoughtful people, the weight of it would become so heavy, it, too, would become a cross. I received special holy cards, pictures of saints and novenas to pray, special cards from religious shrines that promised candles would stay lit for me, and special herbal teas and vitamins poured in by the gallons. I was given more books and articles about healing than a person could ever read in five lifetimes. I could have started my own little store. But I looked at all these gifts that were focused on my healing and I thought, "Why not? Bring it on!"

The other thing people gave me freely was advice. I heard about so many people's relatives who had cancer "just like mine." So many well-intentioned individuals would come up to me and tell me about someone they knew who had cancer and what I needed to do to be healed. I received some good advice and medical referrals. And I received some not so good advice as well.

I felt so much love, and yet so much confusion.

People told me about places to go, people to see, special doctors, clinics and healers to contact. Little by little, I tried many of these things until I finally realized that I would not have time to be a pastor if I were to continue to try each and every healing method sent my way. There simply were not enough hours in the day.

When a person feels desperate and out of control, he is willing to try most anything. This is why one of the best gifts a person can give to someone who is suffering is to be careful about offering advice.

It became apparent to me that I had no idea which one of the many words of advice and healing methods that I had been given would actually lead me to the help and healing I needed. I realized the choices I made in this school of suffering would determine whether I am cured or not, whether I suffer a lot or a little, and whether I live or not. It seemed overwhelming!

And so I did the only thing I knew to do. I went before the Lord and begged him to help me to decide. I said, "Lord, you know I am not smart enough medically, nutritionally, and so on. Guide me to do what is right. I am a lost little child. Everyone is telling me what to do and I am afraid I will make the wrong decision. I am afraid, Lord, that right now you may be showing me what you want me to do, but I'm going to miss it."

Then I realized two basic truths:

✦ We are all children of God. And as children, we are completely dependent on God, our Father.

✦ God, like the perfect parent, wants more than we can imagine, to help us, to guide us and to enable us to be our very best.

Before this realization, I had started to feel like my life was becoming a game show. I had been given three curtains to choose from. The Lord was the game show host and he was telling me, "If you choose the right curtain, Jim, you will live. But choose the wrong curtain, and it's curtains for you." But that's not God. That's not who God is.

We must remember that. We are children. God is the perfect parent who is always offering his hand to guide us on the right path. The tricky thing is that, like a child, we want immediate answers. But God, the parent, doesn't lay it all out in one day. It takes time. It takes time to learn through his Spirit. But God does speak to us. God speaks to us through the language of the Spirit. God speaks to us through the signs of the

39

Spirit. God speaks to us through the ways of the Spirit.

As soon as I realized who I was (very dependent) and who God was (a most helpful and loving parent), only then was I open for learning these ways of the Spirit and how God directs us all.

One of the first gifts that God gave me in this cancer journey was a spiritual companion/director, who for me has become my soul friend. I had been feeling the need to have one special person to help me work through all my thoughts, feelings and struggles with my cancer. So I asked God to lead me to the right person. It was about that same time that my good friend, Father Michael Sparough, offered to help me in any way he could. I recognized Michael's offer as an answer to my prayer.

I began to share with Michael, my friend of twenty-five years, my deepest questions, my darkest doubts and my most awful fears. Michael became the voice of God's Spirit for me, helping me to sift through all this stuff—feelings, advice, messages, all the pressing decisions—and there were so many decisions to be made each day.

Michael quickly realized what was happening and he made a promise to me. He promised to always walk with me, to always be my companion on this journey. With the simple words of a precious promise, this Jesuit Father became my soul brother.

This was amazing, because, before my cancer, I would kid Michael that he would never return my phone calls. Now, he promised me he would always be available to me. His schedule is always wide open for me. Even though he is in Chicago and I am in Cincinnati, I talk to Michael once a week for about an hour. It did not take him any time at all to recognize his role with me in the school of suffering.

This is such an important point. If God is calling someone to be a companion amid suffering, the person must understand the great responsibility this represents—just like Michael embraced his role with me. Sometimes I feel guilty taking up so much of Michael's time, but he is the one who always keeps the connection going by setting up the next conversation before the present one ends. And he keeps reminding me what a blessing this is for him.

It must be nearly impossible to muddle through cancer alone. I found I needed the Holy Spirit and someone through whom the Holy Spirit would work to guide me. When I chose Michael, I did so because he is able to listen well, able to keep confidentiality, and is wise, loving and compassionate. What I have learned through my relationship with my friend is that this is the foremost way in which the Spirit guides me.

If I had to describe the relationship between Michael and me, I would have to refer to Scripture. I have often felt like we were the two disciples on the road to Emmaus. Like those disciples walking along the road to Emmaus, devastated by the death of Jesus, so too, am I walking along my road of life, devastated about this cancer. Michael walks alongside me, devastated about this cancer as well. During this journey side by side, we discuss these feelings and the many struggles associated with this disease. Whenever we talk, we always begin with a prayer to invite Jesus to join us in our conversation. I always believe Jesus does. And, like the disciples on the road to Emmaus, joining Michael on this journey, Jesus has opened my mind to understand so much more.

It is ironic that right before I found out about my cancer, Michael was with me in the Holy Land for that pilgrimage. One day we actually celebrated Mass in Emmaus. I remember that we turned to each other at that Mass and said that we believed that the Lord has put each of us in each other's lives to be close companions and best friends so that we could help each other on our spiritual journey. It was a moment of enlightenment and encouragement for both of us, to see ourselves as disciples on the road to Emmaus. That is an amazing prelude to the spiritual journey of my cancer walk that would begin a mere two weeks later.

I have been blessed with many wonderful friends. But it is

important to point out that a person really must have only one spiritual director/companion. When we find these special persons, we will know it is right because of the ease with which we will share deepest joys and sorrows. Like the two disciples, we all can experience the Lord in our sharing.

For most people, this may not be so much as a spiritual director/companion, but more of a "soul friend." In fact, this term more accurately describes my soul brother, Michael. This soul friend, or companion, more than anything, will be the way that the Spirit of God will guide, support and help a person who is struggling. The soul friend helps a person to filter the inevitable advice that comes from so many places. The soul friend will be that one person to talk it through, think it through and pray it through with us.

My soul brother has been an incredible blessing to me. To my surprise, Michael has told me repeatedly that I am a blessing to him. He has wisely pointed out to me that it is a gift to be able to share in someone's life journey and their vulnerability. This sharing of one's life journey and vulnerability can be especially hard for men.

It is especially hard for Michael, who lost his dad to cancer two years ago. Truthfully, before the cancer took Michael's dad, Michael lost his dad to his dad's need for privacy. At a time of crisis, we often are tempted to close in around ourselves and not let anyone in. Michael's dad chose this kind of withdrawal to deal with his fear and anxiety of having cancer.

By walking with me on my cancer journey, Michael tells me he can begin to find a peace that helps him close the gap left open by his father's death. When one person helps another heal, they both can find healing.

To see God in action like this is amazing. It is so clear that the way God helps us is through each other. So many times I have prayed, "Why don't you help me, Lord?" And the Lord responds, "I will help you through another person." This is the way of healing. It heals our hearts, our souls, our minds and our bodies.

I have come to learn that the school of suffering—as the name would suggest—is incredibly hard to get through. Without a special friend or companion to walk along the way with us and share our struggles, we would not learn some of the greatest lessons of life.

## LESSONS

+ When we face any serious sickness or problem, we can expect to feel a loss of control and to be confused.

+ We are all children of God—completely dependent on God.

+ God, the perfect parent, wants so much to help and guide us.

+ We need to share our feelings and concerns with someone we can confide in.

+ God often helps us by sending us special people.

+ When one person helps another heal, both find healing.

## ASSIGNMENT

+ Turn to the Holy Spirit when you need guidance.

+ Ask the Holy Spirit to guide you to the right person to be your spiritual director/companion or soul friend.

+ Try to identify who it is the Holy Spirit is sending you.

+ Share your feelings, concerns and vulnerability with someone you trust.

## PRAYER

*My Lord God,*
*I have no idea where I am going.*
*I do not see the road ahead of me.*
*I cannot know for certain where it will end.*
*Nor do I really know myself, and the fact that I think*

that I am following your will does not mean that I am
actually doing so.
But I believe that the desire to please you does in fact
please you. And I hope that I have that desire in all
that I am doing.
I hope that I will never do anything apart from that desire.
And I know that if I do this, you will lead me by the
right road, though I may know nothing about it.
Therefore, will I trust you always, though I may seem
to be lost and in the shadow of death.
I will not fear, for you are ever with me, and you will
never leave me to face my perils alone. Amen.
—Thomas Merton

CHAPTER SIX

# Required Text

*All scripture is inspired by God and is useful for teaching, for reproof, for correction, and for training in righteousness, so that everyone who belongs to God may be proficient, equipped for every good work.*

2 TIMOTHY 3:16-17

WHEN I FIRST LEARNED I HAD CANCER, people handed me a number of books, articles, videos and audiocassettes about cancer and its related treatment. Although these works looked interesting and might be helpful, the truth was, I had neither the time nor energy to read or review them all. Therefore, I did the one thing I have learned to do when faced with a decision: I prayed for guidance from the Holy Spirit.

I prayed that the Spirit of God—who is the spirit of wisdom and truth—would lead me to read and to view those resources that would be best and most helpful to me. The runaway number-one greatest book that has helped me most is one that I already owned. It is my Bible.

A priest might be expected to say this. But, honestly, when I was struggling with some of my deepest and worst feelings, my first thought was not to turn to my Bible.

When a person is really in the throes of agony, it is hard to know what to do. But, the Bible is exactly where I felt the Spirit guide my attention.

There have been many times when I felt helpless and in need of assurance from God. At those times, the Bible has offered me such blessed assurance that I can go on. At other times, the Bible has offered me blessed guidance and even a challenge that I needed to carry on.

One of the most helpful Scriptures that has repeatedly given me a great understanding about what is going on in my life is the Gospel that was read at my pre-surgery Mass when my friends gathered to pray for me. It is the Gospel of John where Jesus repeatedly asks Peter, "Do you love me?"

I have often said I love the Lord. But when my spiritual companion, my soul friend, Father Michael read the words, "'When you were younger, you used to fasten your own belt and to go wherever you wished. But when you grow old, you will stretch out your hands, and someone else will fasten a belt around you and take you where you do not wish to go.' (He said this to indicate the kind of death by which [Peter] would glorify God.)" (John 21:18-19). I heard them as if for the first time.

When those words were read, it was as if they jumped off the page and landed directly in my heart. It could not have been any more of an instant message, if Jesus had sent me E-mail! I knew that Jesus was saying this to me. I knew I was Peter, and Jesus was telling me he was giving me this cross. Somehow, you just know.

This particular Scripture has helped me so much. It has become who I am and who Jesus is to me. This is what he is asking of me. This is my whole understanding of what is happening.

Scripture has had an unparalleled effect on me. No other

book has guided me so richly, affirmed me so profoundly and comforted me so lovingly. Never in my life has anything had that kind of power to enlighten me to that degree or lead me in that way. There is no other book that can do for me what the Bible can. The Bible can touch us and teach us in many ways.

One Gospel story that continues to touch and teach me, especially during my school days of suffering, is the story of Jesus on the cross between two criminals also being crucified. The first criminal was on Jesus' right side, while the other was on Jesus' "wrong" side.

The man on the "wrong" side of Jesus blamed Jesus for not taking him down off his cross. Clearly, he was very bitter. The man on the right side of Jesus—with the right attitude—did not blame Jesus. He took full responsibility and blamed only himself. He didn't ask to be taken down off his cross, but rather he asked to be lifted up with the Lord. While the one thief cursed Christ, the other one blessed him. And he simply prayed, "'Jesus, remember me when you come into your kingdom.' And He replied, 'Truly I tell you, today you will be with me in Paradise'" (Luke 23:42-43). It is amazing to realize that this good thief became a saint—canonized by Jesus, himself. The renowned Bishop Fulton Sheen once said, "We call this man the good thief, because he stole his way into heaven."

This powerful Gospel story comes to me often when I think about the crosses we, too, are asked to carry. When we are faced with a cross, we find ourselves at a crossroad in life where we have to choose between the right side or the wrong side of Jesus. At that moment, we choose whether to take the road that will lead us to be bitter or better. Admittedly, it is so easy to get on the wrong side and blame God, others and ourselves. But we eventually discover this does us no good. It only brings us further down.

If we choose to be on the right side of Jesus, we must continually work at developing the right attitude about our suffering. Then we can imitate the good thief by looking to Jesus and praying, "Jesus, remember me," or "Jesus be with me," or "Jesus, help me." Or simply call on his name—Jesus—which means Savior.

Typically, as was the case with the good thief, Jesus does not take us down from our cross or remove it, but he instead lifts our spirit with his and offers us the peace of paradise. This peace of paradise, however, is hard to hold on to in the school of suffering.

Early on in my struggles with cancer, I was caught up with many of the fears and anxieties that go hand in hand with cancer. I would be so tempted to think, "Renal cell cancer, once it has metastasized, is rarely curable." As long as I had to look at that fact, I felt myself slowly sinking into a type of depression. There were so many questions that became distractions. "What about this treatment?" "What about that clinic?" "How about this medicine or chemotherapy?"

I became so overwhelmed that I started to feel like I was actually losing my equilibrium. I thought I was going crazy. I cried out to God, "Lord, I am afraid I'm going to lose it. You've got to help me, Lord. I'm sinking here." At that very moment I felt incredibly drawn by that interior instinct we all have. And this instinct led me to pick up my Bible.

This is a step that I highly recommend for everyone, especially when we are feeling the need for counsel, directions and answers to our questions. I further suggest that we need to first pray to the Holy Spirit to guide us to that special passage that will provide the answers and insights we need.

Second, we need to pray to the Holy Spirit to help us understand and interpret the passage correctly and appropriately for our situation. That is what I did when I picked up my Bible and turned to the story about Peter walking on the water (Matthew 14:22-33). As I have said, I have always felt a connection to Peter and this story is one of my favorites. In this Gospel episode, Peter saw Jesus walking on water. Upon seeing him, Jesus invited Peter to come and do the same—walk on water.

For one brief and beautiful moment of complete faith, when

Peter was only looking at Jesus, trusting in him, he was able to step out in faith and walk on water. Peter was able to rise above the elements of nature. The wind, waves and water could not bring him down. But then, Peter naturally looked down at the frightful elements that surrounded him. As soon as he looked down, he started sinking. When he took his focus off the Lord, he was overcome. So, Jesus reached out his hand to Peter and brought him back to his boat. Then Jesus reprimanded him by saying, "Where is your faith?" (Matthew 14:22-33).

To me that is amazing. Wouldn't we be tempted to say, "What do you mean, 'Where's my faith?' I thought I did pretty good for one moment."

Already, I knew I was in this story. I knew this was not just his story, but it was my story. This is the power of the Living Word of God. God truly speaks to us about our lives and what we need to hear.

I had been saying all along, "Jesus, do you know what it's like to have cancer? I have to constantly face the fact that all information points to the probability that I am going to die! Do you know what it is like to be constantly overwhelmed with these questions and concerns—that, like the wind, come against me with such a strong force that I am overcome with anxiety?"

And I heard Jesus say to me, "Where is your faith?"

I came to realize that if I could keep my eyes—my sole focus—on Jesus, only then would I be able to overcome the natural tendency to be overcome by outside elements and fears—the winds and waves of worry.

When I finished reading this passage, I felt the Lord reaching out his hand to me, just like he did to save Peter from drowning. I felt that! He was saving me. It was as though I could hear him say, "We can learn how to do this together."

The lesson was clear. Jesus was helping me overcome the natural elements. The nature of his power is far more powerful than human nature. And he was offering to me that power— that supernatural power. He was teaching me—step by step— how to walk in faith.

For that reason I think of this story often—especially when I tend to feel down and catch myself looking down at the overwhelming elements around me. In my office, I even have a picture depicting this famous biblical scene. Being able to actually see Jesus grasping the hand of Peter, saving him from drowning, helps to remind me that Jesus is always there—reaching out his hand to us all. We just have to keep our focus on him.

I remember another time when my focus was on the Lord and I was literally crying out to him. I was in my room and it was a rare time for me in that I impatiently blurted out to the Lord, "I have been very blessed during most of this cancer journey in that I have rarely felt horribly down. But I am telling you—no, I am warning you—I'm slipping fast. I feel so sick and tired. And I am so sick and tired of being sick and tired. I have reached my limit of suffering that I almost feel like giving it up."

I continued to lay it on the line for Jesus, "If you had a 911 number, I'd be dialing it right now. I need to hear you speak to me. I need to know what you think. I need something from you that will really help me."

And then I just cried. I could feel the deep tension and frustration pouring out of my whole body. When I finished crying, there was a palpable moment of silence. I remember having a certain image in my mind. I felt as if I had just poured out my heart and soul to Jesus. And he patiently listened. He knew not to say anything until I had finished. He wisely knew I had to cry it out. He knew only when I was through crying would it be his turn to speak. (Ironically, I would later recognize this technique as the same technique I use as a counselor.)

When I was finally ready to listen to the Lord, I felt this compelling feeling, telling me to pick up the Bible and turn to the New Testament. There was even a bookmark that I can't explain, marking Saint Paul's Second Letter to the Corinthians. It read: "We are afflicted in every way, but not crushed; perplexed, but not driven to despair; persecuted, but not forsaken; struck down, but not destroyed; always carrying in the body the death of Jesus, so that the life of Jesus may also be made visible in our bodies" (2 Corinthians 4:8-10).

When I read that I felt the Lord was explaining everything I was feeling. What is more, it also explained the highest purpose for which I was suffering. It was something no counselor but the all-wise Counselor could tell me. It was precisely what I needed to hear.

He was repeating my words back to me—another technique I have used in counseling before! And then he calmly assured me, "Yes, you are dying, but it's not your body, it's your old self. That's why it's hurting so much. But ultimately, you are dying so that I may live in you now and forever."

This story, along with so many other stories in the Bible, has changed my life. Scripture is the way the Lord speaks to us in the most personal and powerful way. Of course, God speaks to us in many other ways: through people, experiences, nature, memories, tapes, books, etc.

But none of these are as inspired as Sacred Scripture. Nothing else has such divine power to inform us and transform us as the Word of God.

For this reason, I recommend learning by heart a few favorite Bible passages to refer to often. Writing them on an index card and posting them on the refrigerator door, bathroom mirror or bedside nightstand will ensure seeing them often.

I have a friend who has committed many Scripture verses to memory by first writing them on an index card and carrying them in his shirt pocket, until he has truly learned them by heart. He claims this simple practice has transformed his entire way of thinking and living.

I personally have found it extremely helpful in my life. In fact, whenever things look really bad for me, I refer in my mind to a particular Scripture verse that always gives me comfort: "We know that all things work together for good for those who love God" (Romans 8:28).

In this school of suffering, the Bible has, indeed, offered me a therapy that no medical treatment can offer. It is an amazing textbook. My great concern though, is that the Bible not only be our primary textbook, but even more be a handbook (often in our hands), and especially a guidebook, leading us through this journey of life.

## LESSONS

+ The Bible was given to us by God to enlighten and inspire us.

+ The Lord speaks to us and guides us through Sacred Scripture.

+ The Word of God has the power to inform and transform us.

+ The Spirit will often lead us to special biblical passages that will be the answer or help we need.

## ASSIGNMENT

+ Keep handy a Bible or New Testament translation, like the *New American Bible*, used by many churches, or the *New Revised Standard Version*.

+ Set a regular time to read the Bible and reflect on it.

+ Reflect on those passages that really speak to you.

+ Ask the Holy Spirit to help you understand the full meaning of the passage.

+ Learn by heart your favorite Scripture verses.

+ Like the "good thief" on the cross or Peter who was drowning, pray "Jesus, remember me" or "Jesus, save me."

## PRAYER

### Prayer to the Holy Spirit

*Come, Holy Spirit, fill the hearts of your faithful ones, and set them on fire with your love. Send forth your Spirit and they shall be created, and you will renew the face of the earth.*

# CHAPTER SEVEN

# Examination Week

*[Jesus said,] "Was it not necessary that the Messiah should
suffer these things and then enter into his glory?"*
LUKE 24:26

THIS YEAR, I EXPERIENCED THE LENT OF MY LIFE! During that
pre-Easter season, I became so ill from chronic diarrhea
(a side effect of chemotherapy), that I had to be admitted to
the hospital, suffering from severe dehydration. I lost ten
pounds off my 155-pound frame within a week. There actually
was a point in my hospital stay when I was so weak and in such
misery, that I wasn't sure if I would survive. It was then that I
realized when we face the reality of our death, we begin to understand the greater reality of eternal life and how this life is
simply a preparation for everlasting life.

But still, it's very hard to let go of this life.

And thanks to the wonders of God and modern medicine,
along with my wise oncologist and the caring nurses, I didn't

have to let go of life yet. Finally, after I had spent twelve long and difficult days in the hospital, which totally tested my faith and patience, I was allowed to go home. It was a day I will long remember because it was Holy Thursday.

I was far too weak to celebrate Mass by presiding, but I will never forget being there. The parishioners didn't know I had just been released from the hospital. I weakly made my way out into the sanctuary to sit down at this 7:30 p.m. Holy Thursday Mass. My surprised congregation erupted into applause as they stood up to welcome me home.

I will never forget what their love taught me about the beautiful meaning of Holy Thursday. This was the very night that Jesus longed to celebrate the Passover meal with his disciples. As I sat absorbing all the love around me, remembering how I desperately had longed to be back with my parishioners while I was in the hospital, I had but one thought, "This must be what Jesus felt for his disciples." This is the very love the Lord invites us to share whenever we gather around the Lord's table.

The next day, I was still too weak from those twelve days in a hospital bed to preside at Good Friday services, but I was grateful to be able to attend and sit through the service. At one point in this service, after reading the Lord's Passion, everyone in church is invited to come forward to touch, kiss or in some way reverence the cross. I was asked to be the first to do this. Slowly, I walked to the cross and gently, I kissed the cross. Immediately, tears welled up in my eyes. As I returned to my chair, I began to observe others process forward to embrace, kiss, or bow before the cross. And I continued to cry. This whole procession took about half an hour. Tears of emotion poured out of me the entire time.

What was it that made me so free to share my tears in that way on that day? "Why am I crying like this? What is going on in me?" I wondered. I had never cried like that at any service in my parish, except perhaps at a funeral. And then it became clear to me.

This cross of Jesus was becoming so real to me. In fact, it

had become the focal point of my life. This cross that I was asked to kiss was a cross that I both dearly loved and yet despised. This cross was my cancer. I was still struggling to accept it as the way I would follow Jesus in his suffering and very possibly in his death.

I had just spent two weeks of hard and bitter suffering. I felt as if I was being told to not just accept the cross but to also embrace and "kiss the cross." All the while I just wanted to trade it in. "Can we talk, Jesus?" I wanted to ask. "I'll take anything but this cancer. Anything. By the way, why do we call Good Friday 'good'? What's so good about all of this?"

I knew that the only answer was "yes" or "no." The question was "Will you go all the way with me?" I was crying because it hurt so very much to say, "Yes." I knew that was the only answer I could give. But it hurt so much.

So that night I prayed for God's strength to help me carry this cross wherever it would lead me. And once again, I surrendered my life entirely into God's hands, trying to imitate Jesus on his cross who uttered a loud cry and said, "Father, into your hands, I commend my spirit" (Luke 23:46).

When I saw my parishioners kiss the cross as well, I was reminded of the heavy crosses they also carry. I then prayed for each one of them, and as I prayed for them, I began to understand that their cross would also be their way to grow closer to Christ and to learn how to surrender their lives to the Lord.

I realized that night that I have attended over forty Good Friday services in my life. Of those, I have led over twenty-three as a priest. But never have I participated so actively, even though I had to sit through the whole service.

The day before Easter Sunday, Holy Saturday, I felt a bit stronger, but I knew I was not strong enough to preside or preach at the Easter Vigil service where we received twenty-seven new members into the Church. The only thing I had the strength to do that night was to lay my hands on each one of them and confirm them with the gift of the Holy Spirit. It seemed so providential that this was all I was able to do, since these last few months I had become painfully aware that the gift of the Holy Spirit is how we find strength in our weakness. That evening confirmed in me the realization that the more aware we are of our weakness, the more open we can be to the Spirit being our strength.

The next day, Easter Sunday, I felt strong enough to both preside and preach at Mass. This was the first time I had been able to do this in quite a while. I was able to tell my parishioners what I believe is the great mystery and paradox of Good Friday and Easter Sunday.

I confessed that this was the hardest Lent of my life, but for that very reason, it led me to my best Easter ever. I preached, "After every Good Friday, there comes an Easter Sunday." For we can never experience one without the other. We have to die with the Lord, in order to rise with the Lord. We have to suffer with the Lord, if we want to share the glory of the Lord.

I felt the Lord was doing this in my very own body and life in order that I could share that with the whole Church. Those words about dying with Jesus that I had been led to when I had cried out to the Lord came back to me now. I knew I was experiencing the death of Jesus. I was reminded that the dying of Jesus was taking place in me so that I could experience the life of Jesus.

As I shared this good news with my parish, I could tangibly feel their spirits being lifted up, too. I realized that our risen Lord wants to continually raise up our hopes and our hearts. His Spirit raises our spirits, as he forever reminds us, "After every Good Friday, there comes an Easter Sunday." I will never forget that Easter. It was my greatest Easter ever.

Whatever we surrender to the Lord, the Lord gives back. Whatever we offer up to the Lord, the Lord blesses us a hundredfold. What I want to say to every suffering person is that suffering never should be wasted. Never. The worst thing that could happen to us is not that we would suffer, but rather that we would waste our suffering or simply endure it. Instead, we should grow from it, and learn from it, and let it unite us to the Lord.

After Easter, I knew I really needed a retreat. I usually try to take two retreats a year—one after Christmas and one after Easter. I usually take five days for this retreat.

So I made plans to visit the Abbey at Gethsemani, a Trappist monastery in Kentucky. I arrived disappointed: I was already a day late from trying to catch up my workload from my time in the hospital and I needed to return a day early for my scheduled chemotherapy session. I had only five precious days and already it was cut short to three.

I cut right to the heart of the matter in my prayer. I said, "Lord, my time here is short and I so badly need to be revived. You know I have been through a very tough time. It took so much out of me. Yes, I had a wonderful Easter Sunday, but, Lord, I need more to revive me physically, emotionally and spiritually."

I arrived at Gethsemani on a Tuesday afternoon. On Wednesday morning, I went to early morning Mass with the monks. One of the priests read the Gospel story of the two disciples on the road to Emmaus. As soon as he started reading this, I started choking up. Something was beginning to stir deep within me. I had always loved this story, and lately it had reminded me of Father Michael and me, but I had no idea why it was now touching my soul so deeply.

Soon I was fighting back tears and feeling self-conscious about letting the monks know that I was losing control of my emotions. I knew enough to know that I had to go pray about it the first chance I had. I went to the chapel. It was time to talk to the Lord about all that was going on in me. "Lord," I began, "what's going on, here? Why is this affecting me in this way?"

So many times we forget that step. So many times, especially when we suffer, we forget to find out why something affects us in a strong way. I've learned that if something touches us deeply, there is a reason for it that may not be immediately obvious. It is vital to reflect on this more deeply and ask for God's Spirit and understanding.

I looked up the verse that had struck me so strongly at Mass, Luke 24:13-17, and I began casually reading along: "Now on that same day two of them were going to a village called Emmaus, about seven miles from Jerusalem, and talking with each other about all these things that had happened. While they were talking and discussing, Jesus himself came near and went with them, but their eyes were kept from recognizing him. And he said to them, 'What are you discussing with each other while you walk along?'"

The story goes on to explain how they were shocked that he appeared not to know what had just happened. They then proceeded to tell him about the events of Jesus' certain death but questionable resurrection.

What struck me first about this part was a line one of the disciples spoke referring to Jesus' untimely death: "We had hoped that he was the one to redeem Israel." That line really moved me because I had faced that feeling over these last several months dealing with my own dashed hopes and dreams in light of my terminal disease. I could truthfully tell the Lord that I had been hoping that I was going to be a great priest and live a long life. I wanted to be a preacher and pastor who would inspire many people. But now, I wanted to ask Jesus, "Are you just going to let me die, now?"

With that connection to the story, the words written on the page, for me, began to come alive. Suddenly, I was one of the disciples having a heart-to-heart talk with Jesus. As I imagined myself walking and talking to Jesus, it became very clear to me that this walk—this journey—was my journey with cancer.

Like the two disciples, I was feeling terribly discouraged. When they talked to Jesus and said, "What do you mean you don't know what's been going on here?" and Jesus told them to tell him about it, I started to actually take over the conversation.

I said, "Jesus, do you know what has been going on in my life lately? Do I need to tell you? Do I need to break this down for you? Do you know all that I've been through?"

And just like his response to the disciples, he responded to me by saying, "Well, tell me."

So then I began to tell Jesus what had been going on in me.

It is interesting to note that I knew, deep inside that Jesus already knew what had been going on in my life. But like the perfect counselor he is, he knew I had to say it. He knew I had to get it all out. And boy, did I get it all out.

Losing track of the time, I cried. Never before had I been so prone to tears. But here I was letting loose the deepest pain that had been bottled up in me for a long time. I let out feelings that I had never before let myself feel, much less express. I said things like, "Do you really care about me? Do you care about what I feel? Does it matter to you that I'm going through this? Does it even matter to you that thousands of people are praying for me? Does this make any difference?"

I was amazed at what was coming out of me. This was raw, uncensored prayer. It was deep, heartfelt prayer. Although I tell everyone to pray this way—"heart-to-heart" conversation with the Lord—it is not easy to pray this way. But this time I had really let loose.

I continued venting to the Lord. I said, "The truth of the matter is I do believe you are with me, Lord. But I don't know what difference it has made. Can you tell me what has changed? And why didn't you let me figure out I had cancer before it had spread to my lungs? You say you help us out, but I would think you would have told me earlier that it was time to go to the doctor! It isn't like I'm hard to get in touch with— we spend time together every day, praying...." I just let it all out.

"And why is it that every treatment I have taken hasn't worked? And why did you let me go through those horribly difficult treatments when you knew all along they would not work?"

Even I was surprised at what was coming out of my mouth. These were things I had never before let myself think, let alone say, because I had always held firm to the belief that God is a good God and is always loving and helpful and we shouldn't be angry at God.

But now I was angry and I told Jesus things that I never thought I could say, because it was indeed, everything I felt. It was everything—the good, the bad and the ugly. It was as if I was throwing up. It just kept coming. I told God things that I felt that I had never before known I even felt. This went on for two hours! I honestly thought my eyes would run out of tears. Only then could I manage to stop long enough to ask, "So, Lord, do you have anything to say for yourself?" What came into my mind was that the Lord was responding to me by saying, "Yes. You need to take a break. Then come back and we can continue this conversation."

I knew that was a good idea. I was emotionally and physically drained. I had said everything I possibly could have said. I had no more words or energy. So I went back to my room and wrote in my journal what I had just experienced. Writing down our thoughts and feelings—especially when we are hurting—is vital to healing. Then I took a nap. I slept for an hour and a half. When I woke up, I felt refreshed. I washed my face and took a little walk.

While I was walking, my mind focused on what had just happened. But trying to pull my attention away from these deep thoughts was a sharp pain in my right knee. My knee had been acting up for quite a while. I pushed the thought of pain aside, though, as I walked back to the chapel. I couldn't wait to hear what it was the Lord would now tell me.

I went into the chapel and I said, "Okay, Jesus, it's your turn. Go ahead and tell me honestly whatever it is you want to say to me." I was half-afraid to hear what it might be. I was moved to pick up the Bible again. I realized that I had never gotten past the first half of the Emmaus story.

As I read the next part, I began to focus on the presence of Jesus, imagining again, that I was walking and talking with him. I also imagined Jesus starting the conversation with me by saying, "Thanks for what you shared."

Wow! Jesus was thanking me! After all I had said, he responded with, "Thank you." He had been waiting for that because he knew I had been holding it in for so long. He knew it had to come out. I just wasn't expecting such a compassionate response.

Then, as I read the story, I, too, could imagine Jesus was saying to me what he said to the two disciples: "What little sense you have." At that I said, "What do you mean?"

I realized that Jesus was simply saying I don't have this greater understanding of life and this all-encompassing view of why he lets things happen in the world. This is when I felt him directly answer me in the Scripture, "Did you not understand that you had to undergo all of this so as to enter into my glory?"

I asked what that meant. He said, "You had to go through all of this first." He then made clear to me that there were many ways that I could have suffered and "died to myself." But he knew this was the best way, this way of the cross, this cross of cancer.

In my ongoing reflection, I felt Jesus explain to me, "Jim, you know you have a strong ego and a lot of self-confidence—some of it is healthy and some of it is not so healthy. Because you like to be in control, you know how you like to have things your own way. All of this must be purified if you want to share in my life and love.

"Just as you understand that no one lives and still goes to heaven, so, too, must you understand that in order to live in me, you must die to yourself."

Jesus continued, "Don't you see how all of this has really humbled you? Don't you understand that all of this has brought you to a point of complete dependency on me, where you learn what an infant child you are before me?" Jesus explained it in a way that all of it seemed right and good. All of it happened for a greater purpose.

I thought, "My God, this is incredible! Everything I said was the most horrible thing that could happen to me, and you are now saying it is all the best that could happen to me."

My attention was then drawn to Jesus on the cross. And I understood.

Jesus' passion and death, indeed, the worst thing that could happen, turned out to be the best thing that could happen. The worst moment in human history became the greatest moment in the history of our salvation. Only then could I truly understand the great mystery and paradox of Good Friday and Easter Sunday. The killing of the Son of God became the redemption of the whole human race. The hour of total defeat and death and disgrace became the hour of God's greatest glory.

So now I understood why we call Good Friday "good" and why all this that had happened to me was also for the greater good. This was a lesson I had to learn. I could only learn it by experiencing it, by sharing in Jesus' cross.

This was a lesson I will never forget. Unfortunately, though, my lessons in the school of suffering were far from over. I was only beginning to listen and learn.

## LESSONS

✛ After every Good Friday, there comes an Easter Sunday.

✛ The worst suffering is wasted suffering.

✛ The Lord wants to help us with our cross.

✛ The Lord wants us to share in the "mystery" of his cross and resurrection.

✛ It is important to have heart-to-heart conversations with the Lord.

## ASSIGNMENT

✛ Allow your suffering to teach you.

✛ Allow your suffering to help you grow and unite you to the Lord.

✛ When you pray, have a heart-to-heart conversation with the Lord.

✚ When you pray, listen to the Lord in the ways that he may respond, for example, through people, Bible, experiences.

✚ Keep a journal of all your thoughts and feelings.

## PRAYER

### PRAYER FOR UNION WITH JESUS

*Come to me, Lord, and possess my soul. Come into my heart and permeate my soul. Help me to sit in silence with you and let you work in my heart.*

*I am yours to possess. I am yours to use. I want to be selfless and only exist in you. Help me to spoon out all that is me and be an empty vessel ready to be filled by you. Help me to die to myself and live only for you. Use me as you will. Let me never draw my attention back to myself. I only want to operate as you do, dwelling within me.*

*I am yours, Lord. I want to have my life in you. I want to do the will of the Father. Give me the strength to put aside the world and let you operate my very being. Help me to act as you desire. Strengthen me against the distractions of the devil to take me from your work.*

*When I worry, I have taken my focus off you and placed it on myself. Help me not to give in to the promptings of others to change what in my heart you are making very clear to me. I worship you, I adore you and I love you.*

*Come dwell in me now.* **Amen.**

# CHAPTER EIGHT

# Being Held Back

*"Now faith is the assurance of things hoped for, the conviction of things not seen."*

HEBREWS 11:1

**D**EMONS. WE ALL HAVE THEM. Throughout my life, one of the worst demons that I have fought is discouragement. By nature, I am optimistic and enthusiastic. I work hard to have a positive attitude. But sometimes when bad things happen, I can become very discouraged. When that happens, contrary voices inside my mind increase in volume and intensity and start to drive me crazy with self-critical, negative and discouraging thoughts. Once I slip into this downward spiral of negative thinking, I find it difficult to pull myself out of it.

We all need to be aware that we all have our own "demons" that regularly trip us up. By the word *demon* I don't necessarily mean something devilish or evil. I define demon as anything that "demeans" or hurts us or others in any way. These demons can often be labeled as an "ism": egotism, perfectionism, materialism, alcoholism, racism, sexism and so on. Or demons can be little sins like impatience, judging others, laziness, apathy, pride, not dealing well with anger, or being overly critical. I have learned that it is extremely valuable and helpful to know and clearly identify our demons. Otherwise, they easily take control of our lives while we don't even understand what is really happening. If I don't know what's wrong, it's hard to make it right.

My experience with suffering tells me that when difficult times occur, in all probability, our demons will appear. They seem to wait to attack, like enemies at battle, in our weakest times and in the weakest areas of our lives, when we are least able to fight back. It is helpful to realize how our demons have power over us. This is a humbling admission because we like to think that we can take care of everything ourselves. Therefore, we need to know what to do or where to go for help.

As I've already admitted, my demon is discouragement, and I have had to fight this continually in my battle with cancer. It is so easy to become discouraged when every other visit to the doctor's office brings nothing but more reasons to be discouraged. I have been more discouraged by the treatment of cancer than by the cancer itself. The treatments bring more suffering and even worse, these treatments so far have failed to heal me.

After the Easter season was over, I continued having more trouble with my right knee. Every time I walked, I could feel a stabbing pain so I went into the hospital for an MRI that detected a tumor in my knee. The treatment for that tumor was radiation. I began a daily radiation schedule that lasted for two weeks. I then had to wait another month to discover through a bone scan that not only had the radiation not worked, but the tumor had begun to erode the femur bone in my knee. At this moment, I was ordered to stay off my leg. Soon I came to know the humbling feeling that comes from being in a wheelchair for a time. Did I happen to mention my demon is discouragement?

Immediate surgery was scheduled for my knee. I felt blessed to be referred to Dr. Joel Sorger, a wonderful orthopedic surgeon who specializes in bone cancer. He performed the successful surgery and was able to scrape out most of the cancer from my right femur bone and fill the hole (which was the size of a small fist!) with a type of cement. He implanted a metal plate to protect the knee and secured the plate with eight large, three-inch screws.

I confess that, although I certainly believe that suffering can be a great blessing, pain medication and the relief it provides are also great blessings. I don't know how I could have survived this knee surgery without such pain relief.

Rehabilitating from this surgery was, indeed, agonizing. By the time I learned to walk on crutches, I faced yet another setback: Three weeks after having my knee operated on, before the pain of the knee surgery had lessened much, another bone scan revealed that two more tumors showed up on each of my right and left femurs at the place of the hip. This new development required yet another serious and painful surgery. I was back in that wheelchair immediately again. Only this time I was warned that if I put any pressure on my hips before the scheduled surgery, I could fracture them, which could do damage that might not be reparable. Because I could not put any pressure on these bones at all, I needed assistance doing things for which I hadn't needed assistance for many years, such as being lifted on to a toilet. I suppose this was just another lesson the Lord was teaching me about how to be like a child.

I had those two troublesome tumors removed, and the surgeons inserted a long rod into each of my femur bones for support. I was again wheelchair-bound for a time before graduating to using a walker. Slowly I progressed to walking with a four-legged cane.

During these somber summer months, my biggest battle was not the suffering from the surgeries as much as it was the discouragement I felt in my recovery and recuperation. That demon of discouragement kept rearing its ugly head. The fear of cancer reappearing somewhere else in my body was not at all unrealistic.

Added to the possibility of finding more cancer was the reality that I would never be as physically active as I had enjoyed being before. For instance, I had always enjoyed playing tennis once a week. Now, following my latest surgeries, my doctor informed me I would no longer be able to play. My demon of discouragement once again loomed. And the possibility of having even more surgeries was more likely than I cared to admit.

Then, less than three weeks after this last surgery, while still recuperating at my parents' home, I was getting out of bed in the morning when I heard something snap inside my leg. This sound was followed by the most excruciating pain I have ever experienced. This pain was so tormenting that I let out a scream loud enough to awaken everyone in the whole house (perhaps, even the neighborhood!). It remains the worst physical pain I have yet experienced.

Upon hearing my outburst of agony, my family came running quickly. They wisely called the paramedics. An ambulance arrived quickly and took me to the hospital emergency room where I would wait, and wait, and wait. While waiting in the emergency room on a hard, narrow wooden stretcher that the ambulance medical team carried me on, I thought only of Jesus nailed onto the wooden cross beam. Although the realization that my pain (as unbearable as it was) could not even begin to compare to the tortuous pain Jesus experienced on the cross, it didn't make my own agony feel any less. But it did help me to again unite my suffering with Jesus on the cross, which encouraged me.

Finally, after five hours of waiting in excruciating pain, the doctors informed me that I had broken a small piece of my *lessor trachantor*, a piece of the femur bone. This bone plays an important role in lifting the leg as in climbing steps. The location of the break explained why it was so severely painful.

Discouragement is so discouraging. I am sure people who have fought sickness, disease or other problems can understand how difficult—and even devastating—setbacks can be. When a person works so hard—day by day, step by step—to make some progress, but then encounters some misfortune that is a setback, it is extremely difficult to deal with emotionally.

Because I recognized that discouragement is one of my weak points—one of my demons—I knew I had to do something. I had to call in reserve strength and extra fortification. And for me that reserve and that extra something is faith.

Faith for me has been one of the greatest weapons against my demon of discouragement. Faith assures me that God is with us: "If God is for us, who is against us?" (Romans 8:31). It is by faith that the greatest saints have overcome the worst sufferings and difficulties. And faith has also helped some amazing people I have had the privilege of meeting.

One of these amazing people came to me during a performance of Jesus' Passion and Resurrection. I had invited Father Michael Sparough to our church to share with my parish and the community this amazing dramatization of the Lord's last days. As I sat in the front pew, I noticed a man arriving late. I found it interesting that he did not seek a seat in the back as most latecomers are likely to do, but instead he walked up the middle aisle to the front pew and sat down next to me. I turned to acknowledge him and was wonderfully surprised to recognize this man: retired Navy Admiral Jeremiah Denton, a former prisoner of war in Vietnam. I recalled that he had spent seven and a half years in solitary confinement suffering indescribable torture. We both turned our focus to the amazing dramatization.

When the dramatic presentation ended, Admiral Denton and I turned to each other. With tears in his eyes Denton told me how touched he was by this dramatization of Jesus' Passion and Resurrection. I understood that here was a man who had shared in Jesus' intense suffering for seven and a half years. He had felt similar agony, suffering and torture. Then, the admiral both surprised and touched me when he said, "Father Jim, I know you and I know that you have been suffering with cancer. I would like to share something with you." With that, Admiral Denton told me a story that inspires me still:

"When I was in prison in Vietnam in solitary confinement, my captor would continually torture me. One day I was tied to a rack. A young soldier was ordered to torture me and break me. During this torture, when I honestly felt I was at my breaking point, a beautiful prayer came instantly to my mind, even though I wasn't praying. The prayer was 'Sacred Heart of Jesus, I give my life to you.' So, I prayed that prayer over and over again. The more I prayed it, the more I felt I truly was giving my life to the Lord. Then this peace came over me like a warm blanket, and I no longer felt pain—only peace. The soldier torturing me saw this transformation in my face and stopped his torture. He went to his commanding officer and said, 'I'm sorry. I can't do this.' And they let me go back to my cell. From that day on, I continued to use that prayer of peace, 'Sacred Heart of Jesus, I give my life to you.'"

I was so moved by Admiral Denton's incredible story of faith that I said to him, "Admiral, I believe that Jesus is speaking through you to me right now. I promise you, I will pray that prayer every day."

Looking straight into my eyes, he answered, "I know you will. And Father, when you pray that prayer, whether you suffer a little or a lot, whether you live a long or short life—it will not matter. You will be at peace."

Since that moment, I have prayed that prayer every day and all throughout the day. Sometimes when I feel I am being tortured by cancer and I am extremely alone, at my breaking point, I remember that prayer: "Sacred Heart of Jesus, I give my life to you."

Faith gives us strength in our weakness. Through this faith, I find true peace. This is something I have employed in my life to aid me in my moments of discouragement. It is a fact that when we are suffering, the evil one knows our weaknesses, and it makes sense that the evil one would try to get to us by coming through our weaknesses, through our demons. That is why it is so important that once we know our demon—our area of weakness—we also need to know what to do. We need to:

Admit we are powerless in this area.

Believe in the higher power of God to help us.

Decide to turn this weakness—and our whole lives—over to God.

Interestingly, these three steps are the first three steps of the Twelve Step Program of Alcoholics Anonymous, as well as of many other recovery programs that have saved millions of men and women from their worst demons. I believe at the heart of these three steps there must be an active faith.

How do we keep our faith active? Faith is like a muscle, much as the heart is a muscle. Faith needs to be taken care of, it needs to be exercised, it needs to avoid certain things to be healthy. Just as certain habits like smoking weaken our heart, certain sinful habits weaken our faith. If we are not aware of our weaknesses during our waking hours, these weaknesses may find a way to appear during our slumber. That is why our dreams often can alert us to something we need to know.

This happened to me recently. In my dream, there were fiery darts coming at me from everywhere. I had to run for my life. I sensed that these darts would be fatal if they hit me. I began to run, but as I ran, I knew I needed help in order to survive. I needed something to shield me. But as the darts kept menacingly coming at me, I became so alarmed that I wakened.

I have always tried to pay close attention to my dreams. Just as the Lord guided many people in the Bible through dreams, I believe he continues to guide all of us in this nighttime "sign language" of dreams. Dreams are our unconscious mind presenting to our conscious self (when our defenses are down during our sleep) what we need to know and consider.

The challenge, of course, is to remember these dreams and to know how to interpret them. No matter how scary or bizarre dreams may seem, they are all "user friendly." They may be intended to instruct us, affirm us, correct us or warn us. Dreams are always meant to help us in some way.

As I sat in the dark of the night awakened and alarmed by a nightmare, I began to reflect on the meaning of my dream. I knew it was trying to "awaken" something in me that I needed to know or to do. I tried to replay the drama of the dream in my mind. Only as I did this could I start to understand the various symbols of my dream. What I realized was that the darts seemed to symbolize my fears and I was becoming "scared to death." Facing my fears now, I knew my faith would be my shield and protection. I began to pray, "Sacred Heart of Jesus, I give my life to you." And then I added, "Jesus, I trust in you."

As I prayed these simple, yet beautiful prayers, I indeed felt my fear disappear. Only then could I sleep in peace. Now, whenever I feel fear and anxiety attack me, which is not uncommon when someone has a terminal disease, I simply pray those prayers: "Sacred Heart of Jesus, I give my life to you." "Jesus, I trust in you." Gradually, as I pray them over and over again, like a mantra, I feel my faith shield me from any worry.

Scripture tells us, "With all of these, take the shield of faith, with which you will be able to quench all flaming arrows of the evil one" (Ephesians 6:16).

Faith makes fear disappear. It is vitally important for all of us to identify our demons, our weaknesses, because a weak link can bring a person down in a moment of true suffering. We must pray for the gift to know our demon. Once we know our demon(s), we must identify what will fortify us in our weakness.

Faith can be our shield as well. It's not a dream. It's the truth. The gospel truth.

## LESSONS

+ We all have demons (things that hurt us or others).

+ Our weaknesses have power over us.

+ In times of suffering, our weaknesses or demons will show up.

+ Dreams can be helpful in instructing, assisting, affirming or guiding us.

+ Prayer and faith can be our strongest shield of protection.

## ASSIGNMENT

+ Pray to know your demon(s) and areas of weaknesses.

+ Pray to know how to deal with your demons.

+ Use faith as a shield to protect you.

+ Remember your dreams and try to interpret them.

+ Pray simple yet profound prayers such as "Sacred Heart of Jesus, I give my life to you" and "Jesus, I trust in you."

## PRAYER

### SAINT PATRICK'S BREASTPLATE

*Christ with me,*
*Christ before me,*
*Christ behind me,*
*Christ within me,*
*Christ beneath me,*
*Christ above me,*
*Christ at my right,*
*Christ at my left...*
*Christ in the heart of everyone who thinks of me,*
*Christ in the mouth of everyone who speaks to me,*
*Christ in every eye that sees me,*
*Christ in every ear that hears me.*

CHAPTER NINE

# Classmates

*[Jesus said,] "Again, truly I tell you, if two of you agree on earth about anything you ask, it will be done for you by my Father in heaven. For where two or three are gathered in my name, I am there among them.'"*

MATTHEW 18:19-20

ONE OF THE HARSHEST REALITIES about suffering is that it can close us off from people—even people we are close to. It can close us off from our family and friends. It can even close us off to ourselves.

Sometimes we are embarrassed. We feel so bad and know we don't look our best either. We find it a struggle to want to be with other people when we don't feel well.

Sometimes we don't want to be a burden to others. We don't like asking other people to help us when we know our requests and needs make extra work for someone.

Sometimes we simply lack stamina. We don't feel like

being with anyone because we just don't have the strength. We find it hard, and sad, to tell someone not to visit because we just do not have the energy to talk for even a few minutes.

Sickness and suffering combine dangerously to isolate us from the very people who love and care for us the most. We suffering folks understand this need to be alone at times, but we must take care not to cut off the love of family and friends whom we need to get through difficult times.

On the other hand, for some people, suffering can be the one thing that finally opens us up—our hearts are broken open. In these cases, suffering opens us to new depths within ourselves, depths never before realized. Suffering leads us to deeper levels of our inner lives.

Pain and suffering also have the potential to open us up to other people who share similar problems and pain. Sometimes, our suffering connects us in odd circumstances, like many different pieces of a puzzle that by themselves do not make sense, but when connected enable us a better look at the bigger picture. This is what happened among my fellow patients during chemotherapy treatments each week.

Sitting together with our intravenous tubes dripping chemo into our bodies, we began to share our similar stories. It soon became obvious that we were connected by much more than IV tubing. We shared our common concerns, questions and frustrations. I began to listen and learn so much from my fellow patients. They became my classmates in this school of suffering. We were in this thing together. And together, we could offer each other the hope and help that few other people could.

Even more than that, we often promised to pray for each other every day. In fact, I keep a personal prayer intention list with the names of many of my new friends in need as well as others who have asked for my prayers. This is truly one of the best ways we can help each other—to pray for each other.

This is how I have learned that compassion is one of the deepest gifts of the heart. The word *compassion* means literally "to feel deeply with." Feel deeply with is what we did in that chemotherapy classroom with our IV pools attached to us, incredibly representing the cross of cancer we had all been asked to carry. I, indeed, looked at my chemo-companions to be like classmates.

Regardless of our age, circumstances in life, or even the type or degree of our cancers, we were all in the same class. We were asking similar questions while dealing with similar struggles. All of us were just trying our best to get through this hard course, hoping someday to graduate and move on in good health.

I listened and learned much from my classmates. I became deeply inspired by their struggles, tremendously uplifted by their little victories, and yet, terribly upset by their setbacks. There is a definite class spirit that can be felt in this classroom of life's struggles. This spirit seemed to be very close to the Holy Spirit, who is the strength of the weak and the hope of the poor.

Recent research has shown that when people share common struggles and come together in some effort to support and share in time of trial, it can provide a level of healing and help that no other expert can give. Perhaps one of the many lessons I've learned from my classmates is not that it is necessary to share with everybody all of our problems and pain, but rather that we share our struggles and joys with those we find in the same classroom as us.

Another major lesson I have learned from my fellow classmates is how to look and listen to the subtle signs of suffering. Few people will wear their disease or disability like a badge or nametag. But you can't miss its identification written in the painful *eyes* of those who are hurting.

My suffering opened me up to recognize how many, many people are hurting: quietly crying, privately pained or secretly suffering. This hurt, this pain, can be physical, emotional, relational or even spiritual. I feel genuine empathy for my fellow classmates, more than I ever could have if I had not suffered along with them.

I carry no illusion that I can or even should try to alleviate their pain and help them solve their problems. Most people in these situations don't need more advice. They just need someone to listen and care.

Imagine the shape of each of your ears. If you were to join these two shapes together, you would have a perfect heart. The best way to share that heart, to love someone, is to listen to him or her.

Many times, after listening to my classmates, when I didn't know what to say or do, I would simply ask if I could offer a brief prayer for them. This is something we can all do for each other. Even though we may not know how to help someone, we can always be confident that God knows how to help the person.

Through my encounters with others who are suffering, I could feel my heart of compassion stretching and growing along with my desire to help others like myself who carry such a heavy cross.

One of my actual joys during my enrollment in the school of suffering is found in the many loving cards and notes from so many friends as well as people I have never met. I am always so touched when they share with me that somehow my struggle has encouraged them in their own struggle.

The truth is, that is the main reason I wanted to write this book—to share some of the lessons I have learned in the school of suffering, in the hope that they might, in some way, help others who are suffering. I learned this lesson from a saintly man I consider my spiritual father, Cardinal Joseph Bernardin, who ordained me when he was Archbishop of Cincinnati.

The close tie that I have felt with Cardinal Bernardin goes back even farther and deeper. Soon after I was ordained a priest, a young religious sister offered me wonderful advice when she suggested, "If you want to be a great priest, identify someone whom you consider to be a great priest. Then, get as close to him as you can, observe and learn as much as you can from him. And hopefully, his goodness will rub off on you."

In my mind and heart, I immediately identified then-Archbishop Joseph Bernardin. I was blessed to become close to him and learn from him. The greatest lesson he would teach me came much later in life when he was diagnosed with pancreatic cancer and he wrote his beautiful book, *The Gift of Peace*. That witness of his suffering and how he dealt with it has been a source of great consolation in my own struggle with cancer. Although I consider him a classmate in this school of suffering, he is definitely at the head of the class—teaching us all not only how to live, but also how to die.

The sister's advice is good advice for us all. We can all benefit by identifying someone whom we deeply admire and respect. Then, if we try to get as close to them as possible, and listen and learn from them, we will become more like them.

Among these greatest role models we can choose from are the saints. I have loved reading about the lives of the saints and have benefited greatly from doing so. I have discovered one common denominator among all the saints: Every one of them suffered a lot. If we read about saints and share in their suffering, they will teach us so much. Indeed, it would be sad if we failed to learn from our classmates both past and present.

My memory will be forever filled with the mental yearbook of the faces of my brothers and sisters in suffering. While I couldn't possibly write about them all here, they will all forever be written in my mind and heart.

There is my good friend, Bob, from my parish. He found out six months before my diagnosis that he had brain cancer. I marveled at the sense of humor he maintained in his class of suffering. I admired his faith that carried him through the rough journey of his brain tumors. After a year and a half of suffering with him through his treatments, he continues to laugh even though his cancer has affected his mind and memory.

Then there is Joyce, a middle-aged woman who has cancer for the second time. One day, during our shared chemotherapy time, she came up to me and introduced herself. She shared with me that every day she prays for me and she carries my photo in her purse as a reminder to pray for me. I was so touched that this loving woman I had never before met was praying for me. She radiates an inner joy.

Also among my classmates is Father Bill Krumpe. This fellow priest and friend of mine was diagnosed with cancer at the same time as I was. We prayed for each other. Happily, we were comforted by the news that his cancer had gone into remission. But, tragically, the cancer came back with a vengeance and Father Bill died suddenly. His death touched me deeply because, for the first time, I could see myself alongside him.

Unfortunately, that is one of the harshest realities I have learned from my classmates in the school of suffering. This course does not go on forever. Some of my fellow classmates have died. In this way, their deaths have been a "graduation" for them as well as their ultimate healing.

During the beginning of my cancer journey, one of my closest friends who was also my tennis partner came down with a sickness. When John Dugan called to tell me he was in the hospital, we joked about how competitive he was, keeping up with my unfolding drama. But just when it appeared that John was going to beat this first sickness, a second one set in, threatening his lungs. Then we knew this was very serious. In my last conversation with him (even though I had no idea it was to be my last), I shared with John some of the lessons I had been learning in this school of suffering. The biggest lesson I shared was that suffering has the potential to bring us closer to the Lord and teach us more about life than anything else.

I was inspired to hear one week later that John had shared all of this with his family and how his attitude had changed about his sickness. Everyone noticed how John had started giving thanks to God for his suffering because of the effect it was having on purifying his soul. I was amazed at how quickly John had grasped all of this. I understand now that God let him have the accelerated course in the school of suffering in order that he would learn it all so well and so fast.

Still, I cried when I heard that John had died. I cried for the hole in my heart left empty that used to be filled with this friend. But mostly, I cried for John's wife and three small, preschool-aged children. When one of John's little boys would later ask me why God took his daddy before he could say goodbye to him, I had to answer that I just didn't know. Some things we will never understand, this side of heaven.

John's death and the deaths of some of my other class-mates continually invite me to think about my own inevitable death. Of course, those thoughts of death are unusual for someone in their forties, but not for someone with terminal cancer. There have been several times when I thought that my death might be imminent. Each of these times, this idea of death seemed to come to me suddenly, no matter how long I may have been thinking about it.

I have tried to think of death in terms of attaining my great-est goal of being one with God and reaching heaven. But like they say, "Everyone wants to get to heaven, but no one wants to die." Without a doubt, death is the ultimate surrender of one's life to God.

What comforts me is to pray about death. There is a nat-ural fear of the unknown, but prayer helps assure us of what Scripture promises. "What no eye has seen, nor ear heard, nor the human heart conceived what God has prepared for those who love him—these things God has revealed to us through the Spirit" (1 Corinthians 2: 9-10).

I have always enjoyed life and I love my priestly ministry. So it is natural that I have always imagined and hoped that God would bless me with a long and productive life working for the Lord. In one of my many meditations on death, however, I re-alized, "Why should I argue if God wants to give me an 'early retirement'?" With that in mind, I pray as some of the great saints prayed, that God may use me even more after death than he has on earth.

When my doctor first informed me that I might have only

a year to a year and a half to live, it forced me to face death whether I wanted to or not. This led me to pray, "Lord, if I only have a year to live, I want it to be my best year yet." Then with the help of the Holy Spirit, I set three goals for the rest of my life:

+ Love God as much as possible.

+ Help others love God as much as possible.

+ Love others as much as possible.

This simple exercise has helped me learn and stay focused on my greatest mission in life—no matter how long or short that life may be.

We all need to ask ourselves that question: "What would you do if your doctor informed you that you only had one year to live?" (Get another doctor?!) If we do this, we can then be open to discovering the secret to living the fullest life possible.

It's interesting to point out that my meditations on death have surprisingly not been morbid. In fact, they have focused my attention and energy on living life to the fullest. As such it raises the importance of giving my greatest attention and priority to my spiritual life, my immortal soul.

We are made up of body, mind and soul. Of all these, the soul is the most important part of us because it is the only immortal part. Our soul will live on forever.

Unfortunately though, while the soul is the most important part of our being, it is, ironically, the most neglected. We spend so much of life caring for our bodies. We spend so much time taking care of our mind. But, many times, we completely ignore the very core and innermost part of us that will live on long after the others have died—the soul.

Suffering invites us to closely examine our soul. It can both purify and fortify our soul. Suffering sifts out all of the impurities that are not of God's love. Scripture explains this by saying, "I will...refine them as one refines silver, and test them as gold is tested" (Zechariah 13:9). When those who suffer allow their pain and struggle to purify them in this way, they will reach an amazingly higher place of union with God.

Even as our minds and bodies suffer, weaken and sometimes deteriorate, our souls can grow and flourish. But this flourishing cannot be achieved unless we are first emptied of ourselves. It is human nature to be full of ourselves. But there will be no room for the Holy Spirit unless we empty out what doesn't belong. It is imperative that we first be emptied in order for our souls to be filled with God.

This is what can happen in the school of suffering, if you are open to the lessons being taught. And this very well could be the greatest lesson of our lives. It's up to us to learn it now. God knows when our graduation will be.

## LESSONS

+ Suffering can close you off from other people and yourself.

+ Suffering can connect you to others who suffer.

+ The Lord allows us to suffer so that we can develop our souls.

+ Death is the way to eternal life—that should be the goal in our life.

+ The saints, in heaven and on earth, are the best role models for us, especially for dealing with suffering.

## ASSIGNMENT

+ Look and listen to the subtle signs of suffering.

+ Grow in compassion and reach out to those who are hurting.

+ Identify someone you admire, get close to the person, listen and learn from him or her. Pray that this person's goodness rubs off on you.

+ Answer the question, "What would I do if I had only one year to live?"

✝ Read about the lives of the saints and learn from these great teachers.

## PRAYER

### PEACE PRAYER
**(Attributed to Saint Francis of Assisi)**

*Lord, make me an instrument of your peace;*
*where there is hatred, let me sow love;*
*where there is injury, pardon;*
*where there is doubt, faith;*
*where there is despair, hope;*
*where there is darkness, light;*
*and where there is sadness, joy.*
*Grant that I may not so much seek to be consoled as to*
    *console;*
*to be understood as to understand,*
*to be loved as to love;*
*for it is in giving that we receive,*
*it is in pardoning that we are pardoned,*
*and it is in dying*
*that we are born to eternal life.*

CHAPTER TEN

# Progress Report

*"I know that you can do all things, and that no purpose of
yours can be thwarted. 'Who is this that hides counsel
without knowledge?' Therefore I have uttered what I
did not understand, things too wonderful for me,
which I did not know."*

JOB 42:2-3

I HAD JUST WOKEN UP and I knew something was different. It was my head; it felt so sensitive to the touch. It almost tingled. "Now what?" I wondered. I soon found out.

The simple act of brushing my hair would usher in a new phase of my cancer journey, as my brush became a hair magnet, taking with it a clump of my hair. After fourteen months of trying to combat my cancer with various therapies, my hair was finally falling out. This was due to the latest and most intense chemotherapy that I had recently begun. This particular chemo is made up of four specific drugs injected into my body.

These drugs have been selected to try and tackle my tumors because in a laboratory experiment these particular drugs had the best effect on a biopsy sample of one of my tumors. This "chemo-cocktail" is relatively new, but it is hoped that it will be tougher on the cancer than the other therapies. Unfortunately, it is also tougher on me.

Suffering and fatigue have been my constant companions for quite some time now. They are unwelcome guests and just when I think I am going to get rid of them, they move back in with a more forceful presence than before. Fatigue in particular has been so hard to deal with. I still have my duties as a pastor that I love to carry out. But the day-to-day tasks of dealing with this treatment have become my first job. And that's a job with few to no benefits.

Someone once asked me if the fatigue I feel is like having the flu. I responded that I usually could work through the flu. In fact, it would only slow me down a little. But this exhaustion is so debilitating that on any given day, if someone would rush into my room and say, "Get out of here, the house is on fire," I would not have the energy to save myself by walking outside.

The bright side is that now I don't have to waste any energy combing my hair. As I reflected on my reflection that showed my hair beginning to fall out, I knew there had to be a blessing in this hair loss somewhere. So I prayed, "Dear God, as I lose all my hair, please also help me to lose all my pride, and not to lose my sense of humor."

On the first day of my second round of chemotherapy, I was really suffering. I had just received my injection that took six full hours to complete. That night, I was so weak with fatigue that I had to be helped back to my room and into bed. Later, as I lay in my bed, I could not sleep. I was on my back. I prefer to sleep on my stomach. I thought about the simple act of rolling over that I had once taken so for granted, that I had literally been able to do in my sleep. But now I could not gather up enough energy to roll over onto my stomach. I could not roll over all night!

When we are suffering, it is often the darkness of night that sees us at our weakest. Between the physical discomfort and the emotional anxieties, it is a wonder we can sleep at all. For it is during the night when we are left alone, that our fears and doubts echo in the silence of the room.

Every morning that I have been at my parents' home recuperating, we celebrate Mass to start every day. I take great comfort in celebrating this Mass with my family. The morning after that debilitating six-hour chemo injection, we were having our family Mass in my parent's home. With the birds cheerfully chirping outside, my sister began to read the Old Testament reading for that day—from the Book of Job.

I had often heard of this suffering man before, but on that day, his story touched me in a way that I cannot describe. It was as if the Lord himself had entered the room and said, "Jim, you need to hear this." I was so moved by this reading that later on I read the entire Book of Job. It is classic consolation to all who suffer.

Job was a good man. He always followed God's word and lived his life the way he believed God wanted. He was blessed with seven sons and three daughters. He was also the richest cattleman in his town. One day, though, great misfortunes began to plague Job. One messenger rushed to Job and told him his animals had all been driven away and his farmhands were all killed. While he was speaking, another messenger arrived to inform Job that all his sheep and herdsmen had been burned up in a great fire. Before he had finished talking, yet another messenger came to tell Job that all of his camels had been driven off and all of his servants had been killed. Still another messenger arrived to tell Job that all of his sons and daughters had been dining in a house that just collapsed, killing them all. Job fell down to the ground in grief. But he managed to say, "...the LORD gave, and the LORD has taken away; blessed be the name of the LORD" (Job 1:21).

But that was not all the suffering Job would endure. Next to be stricken was Job's health. He was soon covered in excruciatingly painful boils from his head to his feet. Job's friends came to see him. The first one said, "You must be doing something to upset God. You must confess." Job answered honestly that he had not done anything wrong. The second friend said, "Somewhere in your past you must have done something horribly wrong. You must now repent." Again, Job denied any wrongdoing. The third friend agreed that Job had to be at fault somewhere. Job continued to deny that he had sinned against God, but only after much cajoling from his friends was he finally driven to go to God and demand answers for his misfortunes. With this, Job asked of God, "Why is this happening to me?" God tells Job that he will answer his question if, first, Job answers God's questions. God begins:

"Where were you when I laid the foundation of the earth? Tell me, if you have understanding. Who determined its measurement—surely you know! Or who stretched the line upon it?" (Job 38:4-5)

Job bowed his head in humble understanding and replied, "I know that you can do all things, and that no purpose of yours can be thwarted. 'Who is this that hides counsel without knowledge?' Therefore I have uttered what I did not understand, things too wonderful for me, which I did not know" (Job 42: 2-3).

Job realized that suffering is a mystery. There are often no answers. We may never understand it. But the all-knowing God allows things for the best.

In the epilogue of the story of Job, he received back two times that which he had lost. I believe this epilogue is reflective of heaven, our afterlife. For that which we lose here on earth, we receive back many times in heaven.

I so badly needed to hear that! I completely related to Job, whose suffering had become so intense and unending that death itself would seem to be a welcome relief. After a day of suffering such exhaustion and feeling at the end of my proverbial rope, I needed to be reminded of God's mysterious ways.

Some things we just can't understand. For example, I absolutely love preaching—reaching people—moving them to greater levels of understanding. But that is one thing that I have had to greatly cut back on during this cancer journey. I just don't have the energy to preach on a regular basis any more. Sometimes I am tempted to ask the Lord, "Why won't you let me preach more?" Like Job's friends, I want to ask, "Is it something I have done?"

Haven't we all wondered why certain things happen in life? So many times we can be quick to blame ourselves, others and even God. We want answers. But the simple truth is, much of life—especially suffering—is a mystery. We will never know the details of God's wisdom. However, we need to know that just as God always loved Job—though God allowed Job to suffer—Job knew in view of eternity that he would be blessed many times over.

And so it is with us. God always has an eternal view of what is best for us. For this reason, God will allow suffering and hardship to come into our lives to prepare and purify us for life everlasting. And there, God will reward us many times for everything we have sacrificed, so as to enter into glory.

As Saint Paul writes in his letter to the Romans, "I consider that the sufferings of this present time are not worth comparing with the glory about to be revealed to us" (Romans 8:18). For this reason, when we go through those dark days and nights, we must keep our eyes on the well-known light at the end of the tunnel. For us Christians, that light is Jesus, who promises to be with us always. "I am the light of the world. Whoever follows me will never walk in darkness but will have the light of life" (John 8:12).

That is the full purpose of this life—to prepare us for the next life. Our mission on earth should be to prepare our soul for heaven. Our sole mission should be the mission of our soul. How do we do this?

The answer is love. However, we need help to fulfill this mission of love. As loving as we may be, we still love conditionally and not as Jesus would have us love. Most of us can quickly think of one person we find difficult to love. And yes, the Lord wants us to love that person unconditionally, too. This is why we must be purged of all that is not of God. We must be purified in order to enter into the place of perfect and unconditional love of the Lord.

Think about this. If we all go to heaven just as we are right now, it wouldn't be heaven for long. We would bring with us all of our unloving ways—judgment, jealousy, greed, selfishness. And that would not be heaven at all. So we must go through some type of purging of what is unloving in us.

This is the teaching of purgatory. Before we enter heaven, we must be purged of all that is not fit for heaven—that is to say, all that is not perfectly loving. One can assume that this school of suffering that we enter can serve to purify us of all that is not of God. The lessons learned can prepare us for a life with God.

Is it any wonder that so many people suffer so much in the aging and dying process? This suffering is a type of preparation and purification for heaven. If we don't learn these lessons in life's school of suffering, we have to stay after school in a place called purgatory. This belief makes suffering not only bearable, but also purposeful.

I have noticed this purification in my own family. As we have gone through this shared suffering, I see my family growing in love and compassion. I see my parents, along with my brothers and sisters, becoming saints as they sacrifice themselves over and over again to do little and big favors for me. My dad, who prays constantly for my healing, has often commented that my suffering has somehow been a blessing to our family because of the effect it has had on all of us.

One surprise blessing my cancer has given me is the ability to share my feelings with people by three simple, yet beautiful words. Much more than ever before, I now find it so natural and easy to tell my family and friends often, "I love you."

Suffering, indeed, has a way of purifying us all, helping us to grow deeper in "...faith, hope, and love...and the greatest of these is love" (1 Corinthians 13:13).

My family and I had more opportunities to grow in love, as my suffering continued. After two rounds and six weeks of the excruciatingly debilitating chemotherapy, I was scheduled to go back to the doctor to find out the results from my last CAT scan. Truthfully, I had come to terms with a few facts:

I have never heard good news at these types of visits during my cancer journey.

I have never felt that the cancer was gone. It has always grown in one direction and that is to get bigger, never shrink.

I have never felt I was cured.

The tendency for most of us who are awaiting test results that are literally going to affect our lives is to try to talk ourselves into believing it will all be fine. However, I believe that type of positive affirmation falls short of the hard reality that one faces.

Positive thoughts are good to have. But warm thoughts can't change the cold reality that I was told one year ago that I might have a year and a half to live. And so it was that I headed off to my doctor's office ready to receive my news.

Usually these appointments are scheduled for the morning, but this day's appointment was scheduled for three o'clock in the afternoon. That could make for a more anxious day.

But I have learned my lessons in this school of suffering. I have done my homework. Every time I could feel myself tensing up with the anxiety of the unknown, I said the simple, yet powerful prayer that Admiral Denton had shared with me:

> Sacred Heart of Jesus, I give my life to you.
> Sacred Heart of Jesus, I give my life to you.
> Sacred Heart of Jesus, I give my life to you.

Honestly, when I would pray that prayer, I was not afraid. I was not even thinking that the results would matter. That is what Admiral Denton said would happen. He said that whether I live a long life or a short life, whether I suffer a little or a lot, none of it would matter if I prayed that prayer. And that's the truth.

But we all must understand that we can mouth the words, but if we don't really do it, if we don't really give our lives to the Lord, the prayer won't work. We have to do it. We have to see ourselves handing over our lives to Jesus as we pray that prayer.

I arrived at the doctor's office with my brother and sister. Of course, there was an hour delay to see the doctor. Finally, we were called back and the doctor came in. Over the year, the doctor and I had worked out the routine. He knows I do not need or want polite small talk at a time like this. He cut to the chase. "The CAT scan showed the cancer has not grown or shrunk. There has been no change."

Just because we pray that beautiful prayer and hand our lives over to the Lord, it doesn't mean the Lord takes away our human emotions. I felt them. I had been through a horrible time with the chemotherapy. It had knocked everything out of me— my energy, my strength, even my hair. Why hadn't it also knocked out this cancer?

I was disappointed. Deeply disappointed. And that's a wonderful response. It is natural and healthy. We should never be asked to deny what we are truly feeling.

But in spite of my disappointment, I realized I wasn't worried. And that, honestly amazed me. Remember, those are my demons—worry and the need to be in control. What is more— I felt gratitude. I knew the Lord was extending my life and even more, he was in control of my life. I knew it was a gift that I was still here at all.

After taking in all the news of the doctor's visit, I was given a thought that I had not thought of for a long time. Several months earlier, there had been a healing service at Saints Peter and Paul Church. During this service, I asked Jesus to heal me, and I truly believe the Lord spoke these words to me, "I will give you length of days to fulfill this great mission I have given you on earth."

Never in my life have I used the expression "length of days." That and the word "mission" sound like words from the Bible;

they sound like words from the Lord.

Again, I hadn't thought of that service or those comforting words for many months. But at the very moment of the test results, when I was feeling the biggest disappointment, I believe the Lord put that thought back into my head to remind me of something. He does not need me to know how much time he will give me here. He just wants me to know that he will give me enough time to accomplish this mission. God has given us all the time in the world.

It was then that I began to understand that I am being spiritually healed, but not physically cured. The distinction is profound. For all the people who are praying for my healing, I want to tell them that it is happening to me—as I am coming closer and closer to Christ through this suffering. I may not be physically cured yet, but I am, indeed, being spiritually healed.

This is solely a gift of grace—a gift of peace—that the Lord is teaching me, molding me, reforming me so that I would surrender to him. This only comes after we have learned to be humble, to trust in God, and surrender everything to the Lord. This is age-old wisdom. And this gift of peace is there for us all.

As I left the doctor's office, even though I had ambivalent feelings of both disappointment and gratitude, I felt God's gift of peace. The doctor's words, "There has been no change," were beautifully balanced by God's gracious words, "I will give you the length of days to fulfill the great mission I have given you on earth."

I understood the horrible chemotherapy would be beginning again. That was hard. People would want to try and comfort me by telling me, "Don't feel that way." But I have come to realize that you have to express your feelings—anything less is false and unhealthy. We must let people who are suffering express their feelings. For this reason, I honestly say, "I don't want to go through another round of chemotherapy, Lord."

And the Lord responds to me by reminding me with the thought, "This is your cross. Take up your cross and follow me."

The Lord doesn't deny my feelings. He confirms them. No explanations, no pep talk. Simply, "I understand. Now pick up your cross and follow me."

As I held the image of the cross in my mind, I sighed, "This is so heavy. But, Jesus, with your help, I will carry this cross for you." The more I held onto this cross, something began to happen. Somewhere along this course, I moved beyond accepting my cross, to embracing it.

Recently a bone scan revealed another large tumor on my right femur (my thighbone). This necessitated another major surgery to remove five inches of my femur and to put a prosthesis in its place, along with a partial hip replacement. Again, this was a very painful surgery and recovery. It felt like I had to learn to walk with a new leg.

My cross doesn't get any lighter, nor does my suffering get any easier. But as I learn to embrace my cross and believe it is the way I can become one with Jesus, the joy and peace I feel being one with Jesus is actually greater than any physical pain I feel.

The foremost lesson I have learned in my continuing education in this school of suffering is that all suffering can be a blessing, even though it is a most difficult and unwelcome one. Nonetheless, God knows best in allowing these misfortunes to come to us to bring about the greater good.

This life is so short. Eternal life is so long.

We must pray for the patience of Job, who never cursed God during all of his incredible sufferings, but always remained faithful to God. Whatever we sacrifice now, like Job, will return to us many times more in blessings, either here or hereafter.

From the very first day I walked out of my doctor's office and into the school of suffering, I have been a student of the lessons of life. The grueling assignments and tests, for me, continue in this school. One of the most humbling lessons I have learned is that I, indeed, have so much more to learn. Someone once told me, "Jim, you must be earning your Ph.D.

in this school of suffering by now."

But the truth is, it feels more like I've returned to the level of a kindergarten student who is learning the simplest, but most important lessons of his life. It almost feels that instead of growing up, I am "growing down" and becoming more like a child of God. As this child-student, the Lord keeps teaching me again and again these simple, but not so easy lessons to live:

+ Be humble.

+ Trust God completely.

+ Surrender everything to God.

The lessons from the school of suffering are difficult to learn. What a blessing it is that we have a great Teacher!

Jesus said, "Come to me, all you that are weary and are carrying heavy burdens, and I will give you rest. Take my yoke upon you, and learn from me; for I am gentle and humble in heart, and you will find rest for your souls. For my yoke is easy, and my burden is light" (Matthew 11:28-30).

I do not know what my future holds, but I know who holds my future.

## LESSONS

+ Suffering is a mystery.

+ Suffering can be a blessing.

+ What we lose in this life, God gives back many times over in heaven.

+ Our purpose in this life is to prepare for eternal life.

+ Even if we are not physically cured, we can be spiritually healed, which is ultimately more important.

+ In "growing down" we become more like a child of God.

+ In trusting and surrendering to God, God gives us the gift of peace.

## ASSIGNMENT

✦ Pray for the patience of Job. Pray for the faith of Job.

✦ Remember that the Lord loves you and wants what is best for you.

✦ Be humble, trust God completely and surrender everything to God.

## PRAYER

### SERENITY PRAYER

*God grant me*
*Serenity*
*to accept the things I cannot change,*
*Courage*
*to change the things I can, and*
*Wisdom*
*to know the difference.*
*Living one day at a time,*
*enjoying one moment at a time;*
*Accepting hardship*
*as a pathway to peace;*
*Taking, as Jesus did, this sinful world as it is,*
*not as I would have it;*
*Trusting that You*
*will make all things right*
*if I surrender to Your will;*
*So that I may be*
*reasonably happy in this life*
*and supremely happy with You*
*forever in the next.*
*Amen.*
—Reinhold Niebuhr